Top 25 locator map
(continues on inside
back cover)
←

D1785562

CityPack
Boston

SUE GORDON

If you have any comments
or suggestions for this guide
you can contact the editor at
Citypack@theAA.com

AA Publishing
Find out more about AA Publishing and the
wide range of services the AA provides by
visiting our website at *www.theAA.com*

About This Book

ORGANIZATION

This guide is divided into six sections:
- Planning Ahead, Getting There
- Living Boston—Boston Now, Boston Then, Time to Shop, Out and About, Walks, Boston by Night
- Boston's Top 25 Sights
- Boston's Best—best of the rest
- Where To—detailed listings of restaurants, hotels, shops, and nightlife
- Travel Facts—practical information

In addition, easy-to-read side panels provide extra facts and snippets, highlights of places to visit, and invaluable practical advice.

The colours of the tabs on the page corners match the colours of the triangles aligned with the chapter names on the contents page opposite.

MAPS

The fold-out map in the wallet at the back of this book is a comprehensive street plan of Boston. The first (or only) grid reference given for each attraction refers to this map.

The Top 25 locator maps found on the inside front and back covers of the book itself are for quick reference. They show the Top 25 Sights, described on pages 26–50, which are clearly plotted by number (**1**–**25**, not page number) across the city. The second map reference given for the Top 25 Sights refers to this map.

Contents

Planning Ahead

WHEN TO GO

Summer and autumn are peak visiting seasons, with plenty of events. Hotels are busy at graduation time (May, June), and rates go up. In October you will get a glimpse of New England's glorious autumn foliage (better still when you go farther north). The six weeks between Thanksgiving and New Year are full of seasonal festivities.

TIME

Boston is on Eastern Standard Time, five hours behind GMT, three hours ahead of Los Angeles.

AVERAGE MAXIMUM DAILY TEMPERATURES

JAN	FEB	MAR	APR	MAY	JUN	JUL	AUG	SEP	OCT	NOV	DEC
37°F	37°F	46°F	56°F	66°F	76°F	82°F	80°F	75°F	63°F	52°F	37°F
3°C	3°C	8°C	13°C	19°C	24°C	28°C	26°C	24°C	17°C	11°C	3°C

Spring (April to May) is unpredictable, but can be wonderful, with cool nights and fresh days. This is when you can catch the magnolia blossoms in the Back Bay.

Summer (June to August) is normally pleasantly warm, but occasional heatwaves can see temperatures soaring into the 90s.

Autumn (September to November) is warm in September, and crisp in October and November, when the foliage is at its most colourful.

Winter (December to March) is very cold. Even when the sky is blue winds can be biting. Snows occasionally transform the city; a slushy, grey mess inevitably follows.

WHAT'S ON

January *Martin Luther King weekend.*
February *Chinese New Year* (Jan/Feb).
March *Spring Flower Show. St. Patrick's Day Parade.*
April *Patriots Day* (3rd Mon): Revere's Ride is re-created. *Boston Marathon* (3rd Mon). *Kite Festival* (or May): Franklin Park.
May *Harvard Square Book Festival. Boston Pops Concerts.*
June *Battle of Bunker Hill re-enactment* (Sunday before Bunker Hill Day, 17 Jun). *Harborlights Music Festival*

(Jun–Sep): Waterfront concerts.
Boston Globe Jazz Festival.
July *Boston Pops Concerts. Independence celebrations* (week of 4th of Jul): Boston Pops concert with fireworks, Boston Harborfest music festival, and USS *Constitution* turnaround.
Italian feste (street festivals, Jul/Aug weekends): North End.
August *Moon Festival*: Processions in Chinatown.
September *Cambridge River Festival*: Events on the river.
October *Columbus Day Parade.*

Head of the Charles Regatta (3rd week).
Boston Symphony Orchestra: Season Oct–Apr.
November *Christmas tree lighting ceremonies*: Faneuil Marketplace and Charles Square, Cambridge.
Boston Ballet–The Nutcracker (Nov–Dec): Wang Center.
December *Tree lighting ceremonies*: Prudential Center, Harvard Square.
Boston Tea Party (mid-Dec): Re-enactment.
Carol concert: Trinity Church.
New Year's Eve: First Night celebrations.

BOSTON ONLINE

www.boston.com
The *Boston Globe's* website has the daily newspaper, with local news, things-to-do listings, and restaurant reviews.

www.bostonphoenix.com
The *Boston Phoenix* is a weekly alternative newspaper that offers detailed arts and entertainment listings, plus restaurant reviews.

www.bostonusa.com
Run by the Greater Boston Convention and Visitors Bureau, this site includes details about attractions, events, hotels, and the subway, as well as other useful visitor information.

www.cambridge-usa.org
This is the Cambridge Office for Tourism's site and it contains listings of hotels, restaurants, attractions, and arts and entertainment venues, as well as an events calendar and general visitor information for the City of Cambridge.

www.mbta.com
The website of the MBTA (Massachusetts Bay Transportation Authority) is the place to look for timetables, maps, and fare information for the T (subway), as well as buses and commuter rail services.

www.fodors.com
A complete travel-planning site. You can research prices and weather; book air tickets, cars, and rooms; ask questions (and get answers) from fellow travellers; and find links to other sites.

www.massvacation.com
Visitor information from the Massachusetts Office of Travel and Tourism. The site includes an accommodation booking service.

www.orbitz.com
An air-fare search engine owned by five US airlines. It frequently offers low-fare specials.

CYBERCAFÉS

Designs for Living
A combination coffeehouse, bookshop, art gallery, and cybercafé in the Fenway.
➕ E6 ✉ 52 Queensberry Street
☎ 617/536-6150;
www.bosnet.com
◉ Sep–May 8AM–4PM.
Jun–Aug 8AM–9PM
🚇 Kenmore, Fenway
💳 $8 per hour

Mama Gaia's Café
A 1960s-style café in Central Square, offering breakfast, sandwiches, and light meals, along with free Internet access for customers.
➕ D4 ✉ 401 Massachusetts Avenue, Cambridge
☎ 617/441-3999;
www.mamagaiascafe.com
◉ Sun–Thu 7AM–10PM;
Fri–Sat 7AM–midnight
🚇 Central 💳 Free

Kinko's
Copy and printing shops that offer Internet access. Locations include:
➕ F5 ✉ 187 Dartmouth Street (Back Bay) ☎ 617/262-6188 ◉ 24 hours
🚇 Back Bay, Copley
💳 $12 per hour; ➕ C2 ✉ Mifflin Place (off Mt. Auburn Street, Harvard Square) ☎ 617/497-0125
◉ 24 hours 🚇 Harvard
💳 $12 per hour

Getting There

ENTRY REQUIREMENTS

Visitors to the US must show a full passport, valid for at least six months. Most UK citizens and visitors from other countries belonging to the Visa Waiver Program can enter without a visa, but you must have a return or onward ticket. However, as this guide went to press, changes to the entry requirements were being considered. Check with the US Embassy, London (☎ 020 7499 9000; www.usembassy.org.uk).

MONEY

The currency is the dollar (=100 cents). Notes (bills) are in denominations of $1, $5, $10, $20, $50, and $100; coins are 25¢ (a quarter), 10¢ (a dime), 5¢ (a nickel), and 1¢ (a penny). You may find that small businesses will not break a $100, $50, or even $20 bill.

$10

$50

$100

ARRIVING

Logan Airport is on an island in Boston Harbor, 5km (3 miles) from downtown. It has five terminals (linked by walkways and shuttle buses), hotels, and restaurants. Domestic flights also use T.F. Green Airport (Rhode Island), Manchester Airport (New Hampshire), and Worcester Airport (Massachusetts).

FROM LOGAN AIRPORT

For general airport information ☎ 800/235–6426. "Massport Shuttle" buses run every 8–12 minutes (5.30AM–1AM; free) from every terminal to Airport subway (T) station; from here it's a few minutes' journey to central Boston ($1).

Taxis cost $12–$15 (including a tunnel toll, but not tip). There is always rush hour congestion in the tunnels. Allow around 30 minutes to or from Back Bay off peak, and an hour at peak times. The Airport Water Shuttle (☎ 617/330–8680) is an exciting way to arrive in central Boston. It's a 10-minute ride between Logan and Rowes Wharf in the Financial District, where you can pick up a taxi (Mon–Thu 6AM–8PM; Fri 8AM–11PM; Sat 10AM–11PM; Sun 10AM–8PM; no service on certain public holidays; $10 one way). Harbor Express (☎ 617/376–8417) operates between Logan, Long Wharf, and Quincy (Mon–Fri 5AM–10.35PM; Sat, Sun 6AM–9.45PM; $10 to Long Wharf). From April to mid-October an on-call City Water Taxi (☎ 617/422–0392) runs from Logan to ten waterfront locations (7AM–7PM; $10). Shuttle buses connect all terminals with the water taxis.

OTHER AIRPORTS
Domestic flights also use T.F. Green Airport, Providence (☎ 401/737–4000); Manchester Airport, New Hampshire (☎ 603/624–6539); and Worcester Airport, Massachusetts (☎ 508/799–1741). It's then an hour's bus ride to Boston.

ARRIVING BY BUS
Greyhound (☎ 800/231–2222) and Peter Pan Trailways (☎ 800/343–999) travel between New York and Boston's South Station, and (less frequently) to the rest of the USA and Canada.

ARRIVING BY CAR
From the west: Route I-90, the Massachusetts Turnpike, runs into Boston with exits leading to Cambridge, Storrow Drive (for Fenway, Kenmore Square, and Boston Common), the Back Bay, downtown, and I-93 (the expressway). **From the south:** I-93 has exits for Chinatown, South Station, downtown, and for the Callahan Tunnel to the airport. **From the north:** US1 and I-93 have exits marked Storrow Drive (for Cambridge and Boston Common), High Street (for downtown), and Kneeland Street (for Chinatown and the Theater District).
Driving and parking in Boston is a nightmare.

ARRIVING BY TRAIN
Amtrak (☎ 800/872–7245; www.amtrak.com) runs hourly services between Boston's South Station and Providence, New York, Philadelphia, and Washington, D.C. The high-speed Acela service between New York and Boston takes two hours 45 minutes. South Station also serves Montréal and Chicago. Amtrak's Downeaster travels up the Maine coast from North Station.

GETTING AROUND
The best way of getting around Boston is the subway, known as the T. There are four lines: Blue (serving the airport), Red (serving South Station), Green, and Orange. "Inbound" and "Outbound" refer to the direction in relation to Park Street Station. Buy tokens ($1) at the subway stations. Trains run 5AM–12.45AM.
For more information ➤ 92.

INSURANCE
It is vital to have cover for medical expenses, as well as for theft, baggage loss, trip cancellation, and accidents.
Check your insurance coverage and by a supplementary policy as needed.

VISITORS WITH DISABILITIES
An Airport Handicap Van offers a free service between all Logan Airport locations. Use the free "Van Phone" in the baggage claim area. Public buildings, parking areas, and subway stations provide wheelchair access, and many hotels have specially designed rooms. Modern or newly renovated hotels and restaurants tend to be better equipped. For further information contact: New England INDEX ✉ 200 Trapedo Road, Waltham, MA 02452 ☎ 800/642–0249 (in New England) or 781/642–0248.

Living
Boston

Boston Now

Above: *Quincy Market*
Above right: *an autumn display outside the Green Dragon Tavern*

Boston is the birthplace of the American Revolution. No other US city is so rich with history. But it is also a city that has moved with the times—a city of high finance and high-tech research. It is home to the Red Sox and the Patriots, Filene's Basement and Dunkin' Donuts, Italian *feste* and Irish politicians—as well as that famous Puritanical streak that catapulted so many books to the national best-seller lists after they were "banned in Boston."

Boston is one of the most beautiful cities in the country and is also one of the easiest to explore. A day or two's footwork will cover its compact, historic core. If you do tire of walking, or want to

---

NICKNAMES

- **The Hub:** In 1858 the essayist Oliver Wendell Holmes called the Massachusetts State House the "hub of the solar system." The term is now applied to Boston as a whole.
- **Beantown:** As it was against the law for the Puritans to cook on Sundays, they prepared baked beans on Saturdays, a custom which earned Boston the nickname Beantown.
- **The T:** The subway system in Boston is known as the T, a name derived from its operator, the Massachusetts Bay *Transportation* Authority.

FEDERAL STYLE

● Charles Bulfinch (1763–1844) is hailed as having made Boston architecturally. After designing the new State House and 12 churches, he turned to the large-scale redevelopment of Beacon Hill. The neoclassical style he used became known as "Federal." Yet he felt unappreciated, was often in financial straits, and was seduced away to Washington, D.C., to work on the Capitol.

conserve energy for the Fenway art galleries, there is always the subway, known as the T; it's inexpensive, clean, efficient, and easy to use.

Across the river, in the town often referred to as the "People's Republic of Cambridge" for its liberal leanings, are Harvard University and the Massachusetts Institute of Technology. Together, Boston and Cambridge boast more than 60 colleges and universities, and the 250,000 students that descend each September give the place a vibrant buzz.

It is this academic inclination, as much as anything, that has shaped the area since its beginnings. The large number of graduates who come to call Boston home has made the city one of the most affluent and well-educated in the US. It is a must-stop for lecturers, writers, musicians, and politicians, and a permanent base for many of the nation's most original thinkers and cutting-edge scientists and doctors.

Above: a reflection of Trinity Church on the mirror-glass fronted John Hancock Tower
Below: the bat-and-ball sign above Fenway Park, home of the Red Sox

Above: the cobbled paths of Acorn Street, in Beacon Hill

THE BIG DIG

• Boston's sole blight currently is the Big Dig. This project, on a par with the construction of the Channel Tunnel and the Alaska Pipeline, involves burying the elevated Central Artery, Boston's main highway, which currently separates downtown from the North End and the Waterfront. Once buried (in late 2004), it will be covered with parkland, new housing, and retail space, and the face of the area will be changed beyond recognition.

The colleges also attract a large, often transient international population that gives the city a constantly changing face. This lively mix, along with the philanthropic inclinations of the original Boston Brahmins, has made for an energetic and eclectic arts scene.

Boston's cultural life has also benefited from the wealthy residents who visited Europe in the 19th century. Their exceptional legacy is shown in such internationally recognized treasuries as the Museum of Fine Arts, the Isabella Stewart Gardner Museum, and Harvard University's Fogg Art Museum. There is a worthy opera company, as well as the Boston Symphony Orchestra and Boston Pops Concerts, and many Broadway shows premiere in the Theater District. Jazz, blues, folk, and bluegrass keep Cambridge hopping every night of the week and the pop and rock milieu is an incubator for acts like Paula Cole and They Might Be Giants. For sports fans there are those perennial runners-up the fiercely loved Red Sox, basketball and hockey at the FleetCenter, and the relatively new and extraordinarily popular soccer teams The New England Revolution and the Boston Breakers.

Left: *Faneuil Hall Marketplace*
Above: *cannon on the USS Constitution*

Bostonians love the outdoors and on any moderately pleasant day you will find the Esplanade along the Charles River brimming with runners, walkers, in-line skaters, frisbee players, skateboarders, cyclists, and those who simply want to relax with a good book under a tree; outdoor concerts throughout the summer

GETTING YOUR BEARINGS

● Boston Common and the Public Garden lie at the heart of Boston. To their north is the old residential area of Beacon Hill, while to their west and south is elegant Back Bay, where many of the shops and hotels are found. This extends westwards to the Fenway (art museums, Fenway Park, Kenmore Square nightclubs), while the eastern edges of the Back Bay meet the trendy, gay-friendly South End. Southeast of Boston Common are the Theater District and Chinatown, which adjoin to their north the Financial District. The Freedom Trail, which starts on the Common, runs northeast through Old Boston, edged by the Financial District and the Waterfront, past Faneuil Hall/Quincy Market to the Italian North End. Westwards across the Charles River lies Cambridge, with Harvard Square at its core.

CHANGING THE LANDSCAPE

● Beacon Hill is the sole remnant of three peaks on the Shawmut Peninsula; the other two were removed in the early 1800s and used for infill. (Some 58 percent of Boston is built on landfill.) In the mid-1800s swamps on either side of the isthmus were filled in to develop the Back Bay and South End.

Above: *inside the Museum of Fine Arts*
Above centre: *the Boston Pops Orchestra plays at Symphony Hall*
Right: *jogging along the Charles River Esplanade*
Above far right: *Commonwealth Avenue's brownstone terraces, seen from the Prudential Skywalk*

bring even greater crowds. The Charles itself, a glittering oasis that both separates and unites Boston and Cambridge, is dotted with rented sailing boats in all but the most horrendous weather. And even those famously cold New England winters are cause for celebration: Skiing is practically the official state sport, and snow-boarding and ice skating are equally embraced. Within an hour's drive of the city you can find white-water rafting, horseback riding, mountain climbing, hang-gliding, extreme kayaking, surfing, windsurfing, and countless hiking trails.

Whatever you choose to do in Boston, you can't escape the city's history. Eat out in the vibrant Italian quarter, and you will find yourself in a

THE BOSTON BRAHMIN

• The Proper Bostonians, whom Oliver Wendell Holmes called Brahmins after the high-ranking Hindu caste, trace their origins to the wealthy merchants of the 18th and 19th centuries. These families—among them the Lowells, Appletons, and Cabots—were known for their Puritan values, including discretion and frugality (it was said the Lowells spoke only to the Cabots, and the Cabots spoke only to God). The scions of these illustrious families may no longer live on Beacon Hill, but they still call Harvard "Hah-vud."

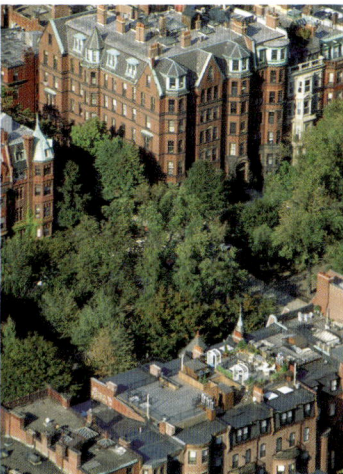

tangle of narrow streets laid out by British colonists in the 17th century. Set off on the Freedom Trail (and you haven't done Boston if you haven't walked the Freedom Trail) and you'll be following a red line on the sidewalk that guides you through significant landmarks of the American colonies' struggle for independence from Britain. Stroll through Boston Common and you'll see the first public park in the US and the archetype of town greens all over New England. If you have come for the architecture, you will surely end up in the elegant terraces of Beacon Hill, built in the early 1800s for the city's elite, or on the grand magnolia-lined Victorian avenues of Back Bay. Yet never out of view are the modern towers of the Financial District, and seemingly at every turn the gleaming glass shaft of the Hancock Tower rises serene and confident above the city's brownstone rooftops. It is this juxtaposition of old and new that is so exciting about Boston.

INVENTIONS

Boston- and Cambridge-based inventors have given us:
- The use of ether as an anaesthetic (Dr. John C. Warren, 1846).
- The telephone (Alexander Graham Bell, 1875).
- The safety razor (King Gillette, 1901).
- The spark plug (Albert Champion, 1915).
- The iron lung (Dr. Philip Drinker, 1927).
- The first computer "Differential analyzer" (MIT, 1928).
- Polaroid film (Edwin Land, 1932).
- The Pacemaker (Dr. Paul Zoll, 1952).

15

Boston Then

Left to right: *the landing of the Pilgrim Fathers; the Boston Massacre; the Boston Tea Party; Paul Revere; State Street c1840*

REVOLUTION

In the 1760s Britain imposed taxes on her New England colonists. Increasingly angry at interference in their lucrative seafaring trade, the colonists, led by Sons of Freedom Sam Adams and John Hancock, protested at having to pay taxes when they had no representation in the government that was taxing them. Tension began to mount and on 5 March 1770 British soldiers killed five colonists in what became known as the Boston Massacre. On 16 December 1773 Patriots protested against the Tea Act by throwing tea into the sea (the Boston Tea Party). British retaliation made war inevitable.

Pre-1620 The Algonquins inhabit the Boston area.

1620 Pilgrims arrive on the *Mayflower* and establish the first English colony in Plymouth.

1629 Puritans found the Massachusetts Bay Colony in Charlestown.

1630 The Colony moves to Beacon Hill on the Shawmut Peninsula.

1636 Harvard College is founded.

1680 Most of Boston is concentrated in what is to become the North End, around the flourishing seaport.

1775 The Revolution starts in Boston.

1776 The British leave Boston on 17 March. Four months later, on 18 July, the Declaration of Independence is read from the State House balcony.

1790s Trade with China brings prosperity.

1795 Architect Charles Bulfinch starts the new State House. Five years later he helps to develop Beacon Hill.

1826 Mayor Josiah Quincy extends the waterfront and builds Quincy Market.

1840s Irish immigrants, fleeing the potato famine, pour into the North End.

1856 Work begins on filling in and developing the Back Bay as a new residential area for the elite.

1877 Swan Boats—distinctive boats with large model swans at the helm— come to the Public Garden.

1880s The Irish make their mark in politics.

1897 The Boston marathon is launched.

1918 The Red Sox win baseball's World Series—their first and only pennant victory.

1957 The first of 16 NBA championship victories by the Celtics.

1960s -70s An extensive urban renewal scheme includes John Hancock Tower.

1990 The US' biggest art theft occurs at the Isabella Stewart Gardner Museum.

1995 FleetCenter replaces the Boston Garden, home of the Bruins (ice hockey) and Celtics (basketball).

2002 New England Patriots win the Super Bowl.

PAUL REVERE'S RIDE

In his lifetime Paul Revere (1735–1818) was known as a silversmith, but he was immortalized—with some poetic licence—as a hero of the Revolution by the poet Henry Wadsworth Longfellow. Revere was a messenger for the Sons of Liberty and on the eve of the first battle of the Revolution rode to Lexington to warn local militia men about British preparations.

J.F.K.

John Fitzgerald Kennedy was born in the Boston suburb of Brookline in 1917. His grandfather, "Honey-Fitz," was one of a long line of Irish mayors. Kennedy was elected president in 1960—good-looking and charismatic, he was a symbol of the nation's hope for a progressive future. He was assassinated on 22 November 1963.

Time to Shop

Below: *Newbury Street, with its brownstone terraces*
Right: *the mall in the Prudential Center*

Some of Boston's best shopping areas are in the city's most attractive neighbourhoods. One-of-a-kind shops selling clothes, books, or antiques rub shoulders with outlets for contemporary crafts, innovative gifts, and home accessories. Newbury Street is a joy, with its boutiques in

ONLY IN BOSTON

Baked beans were invented in Boston by early colonists, who cooked them in molasses (hence the city's nickname, Beantown). Today, red Boston beans (albeit in candy form) are sold on souvenir stands in containers of every shape and size.

The lobster shows up in all the usual touristy guises, from fridge magnets, key rings, and mugs to pencil tops, erasers, and notebooks. As for T-shirts, sweatshirts, and baseball caps, take your pick—they come bearing logos of local universities, like Harvard, and the local teams, including the Red Sox, the Bruins, the Celtics, and, of course, 2002 Super Bowl champions the Patriots.

lovely brownstone Victorian buildings. People travel long distances to shop for clothes here, from top designer labels to the fabulously funky and the "gently used." With the great outdoors on the doorstep, many shops specialize in outdoors gear and clothing.

Like all of New England, Boston is good hunting ground for antiques. Clustered in and around Charles Street, at the foot of Beacon Hill, are dozens of shops. Most are specialists, selling oriental rugs, furniture, porcelain, silver, or antique maps for serious money. Even if you can't afford to buy, it's a pleasure to browse. In Cambridge, hundreds of dealers in two large markets offer cheaper collectables, alongside furniture, silverware, and other antiques.

With academia playing a pivotal role in the area, it is no surprise to find a plethora of

bookshops—new, used, and antiquarian—particularly around Harvard Square. Whether you're looking for a coffee-table book on Boston to take back home, or something rare and erudite, you can browse undisturbed, in some shops until 11PM.

Below left: Quincy Market
Below: end a hard day's
shopping with a drink in the
Bull & Finch, the bar that
inspired the long-running
TV series Cheers

Fine contemporary crafts are easy to find in Boston. Look along Newbury and Charles streets, and in the South End, as well as in Cambridge.

Three or four of New England's big outlets—where clothes, shoes, and household goods are available at discounts of up to 65 percent—are within an hour of central Boston. They make a tempting day trip if you get a buzz from finding a bargain.

At the farmers' markets that start up in autumn in Copley Place (Tue, Fri) and Harvard Square (Sun), you can find all the goodies available around rural areas of New England at roadside farm stands—maple syrup, cheese, and honey, among other things. Only the red-painted barn stacked high with corn cobs, apples, and pumpkins is missing.

UK TRAVELLERS

If you are hunting for a bargain you should look in the malls and chain stores all over Boston, where clothes (except for woollens), leather goods, and shoes are less expensive than back home. You will also find CDs at good prices. Before you let your spending run wild, check the current customs limits for bringing goods back to the UK.

Out and About

ORGANIZED SIGHTSEEING

Boston is hard to beat when it comes to organized tours. For walking tours (guided or self-guided) try the Black Heritage Trail, which explores the history of the African-American community on Beacon Hill (✉ 617/725–0022),

or the Freedom Trail (✉ 617/242–5642). Boston by Foot (✉ 617/367–2345) also organizes guided walks. Trolley Tours include the Beantown Trolley (red, ✉ 617/720–6342), Old Town Trolleys (green and orange, ✉ 617/269–7010), and Discover Boston Multi-lingual Trolley Tours (✉ 617/742–1440). Boston Duck Tours travel through historic Boston in renovated World War II amphibious vehicles, then splash into the Charles River. Tours leave from the Prudential Center (✉ 617/723–DUCK 🕙 Apr–Nov).

EXCURSIONS
PLYMOUTH

The Pilgrims' landing of 1620 (the exact location is debated) is commemorated on the town's waterfront by Plymouth Rock. You can board the replica *Mayflower II*, docked nearby, and tour Plimoth Plantation, a meticulously researched reproduction Pilgrim settlement 5km (3 miles) south, where interpreters in period costume chat with visitors while getting on with their daily chores. At the Wampanoag Indian Homesite, Native Americans—on whose ancestors' land the Pilgrims settled—tell of their experiences.

SALEM

To many, Salem means witches so it's not surprising to find here a range of interpretations of the mass hysteria that hit the town in the 1690s (most notably the Salem Witch Museum). Less well known but far more striking once you're

there is that the town also has a rich maritime history and some of the best Federal architecture in America. In the 18th and early 19th centuries Salem's prosperous ship builders, merchants, and sea captains built graceful houses and filled them with beautiful things. Many of these objects are in the Peabody Essex Museum.

LEXINGTON AND CONCORD

These lovely towns are immortalized by events that sparked the first shots of the Revolution. It was to Lexington, where Patriot leaders were staying, that Paul Revere made his famous ride to warn of British plans to seize a cache of arms in Concord. It was on Concord's North Bridge, on 19 April 1775, that the "shot heard round the world" was fired. Re-enactments take place in both towns on Patriots' Day (the third Monday in April). Concord has a literary past too, as the home of influential early 19th-century writers and thinkers Henry David Thoreau, Ralph Waldo Emerson, Nathaniel Hawthorne, Louisa May Alcott, and her brother Bronson. Visit their houses, and their graves in Sleepy Hollow Cemetery.

INFORMATION

SALEM

Distance 26km (16 miles)
Journey Time 30 minutes
🕐 Peabody Essex Museum closed Mon in winter. Witch Museum open daily
🚆 From North Station
⛴ From Long Wharf
🛈 Destination Salem
   ✉ 63 Wharf Street
   ☎ 877/725–3662;
   www.salem.org

Left: *thatching a roof at the Plimoth Plantation*
Centre: *the entrance to the Mayflower Society Museum, Plymouth*
Right: *the Old North Bridge, spanning the River Concord*

INFORMATION

CONCORD

Distance 32km (20 miles)
Journey Time 40 minutes
🕐 Emerson's and Hawthorne's houses closed winter; other sites open all year. Hours vary
🚆 From North Station
🛈 Concord Chamber of Commerce ✉ 105 Everett Street
   ☎ 978/369–3120;
   www.concordma chamber.org

Walks

INFORMATION

Distance 2.5km (1.5 miles)
Time 1 hour
Start point ★ Beacon Street (by State House)
🚇 bIV; G4
🅿 Park
End point Beacon Street at Charles Street
🚇 bIV; G4
🅿 Park, Arlington
❓ Beacon Hill is steep in parts and some of the streets are cobbled. Wear suitable shoes.

BEACON HILL

Start on Beacon Street at the State House and walk downhill. The Appleton Mansions at No. 39, where poet Longfellow (➤ 26) was married, and No. 40, have some of the highly prized purple panes (flawed originals that are now rare, ➤ 37). At the bottom turn right onto Charles Street, up Chestnut Street, and left onto Willow Street. On the left is a much-photographed view down Acorn Street. Houses in lanes such as this were for servants. Continue to Mt. Vernon Street. The beautiful Louisburg Square, where author Louisa May Alcott died, is ahead. Continue up Mt. Vernon Street and detour onto Walnut Street and briefly into Chestnut to see Nos. 13, 15, and 17, a lovely trio.

Return to Mt. Vernon Street to visit the Nichols House, a family home until the 1960s (➤ 55). At the end of Mt. Vernon, turn left onto Joy Street. The African Meeting House (➤ 55), important in the history of African Americans in Boston, is farther down Joy Street, north of Pinckney Street. Turn onto Pinckney Street, with its fine view of the Charles River. Detour right onto Anderson Street and right again onto Revere Street. The columned facade between 29 and 25 is a trompe l'oeil. Return to Pinckney and follow it down to Charles Street. Return to Beacon Street. From here you can join the Freedom Trail by the Shaw Monument (➤ 57) in front of the State House.

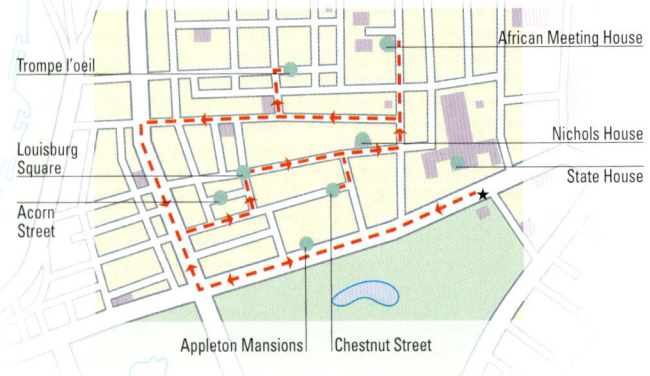

Trompe l'oeil

African Meeting House

Louisburg Square

Nichols House

State House

Acorn Street

Appleton Mansions   Chestnut Street

THE FREEDOM TRAIL TO COPP'S HILL

Start at the information centre on Boston Common and head for the Massachusetts State House (► 40). Walk down Park Street to "Brimstone Corner"—gunpowder was stored in Park Street Church (► 58) during the War of 1812 with Britain. On Tremont Street, in the Old Granary Burying Ground, find the graves of many famous people (► 58). King's Chapel (► 58) is the oldest church site in Boston still in use. On School Street a sidewalk mosaic marks the site of the first free school, open to all. Pass a statue of Benjamin Franklin and reach the Globe Corner Bookstore, a meeting place for 19th-century literati. Diagonally right, past the Irish Famine Memorial (► 57), is Old South Meeting House (► 42), where the Boston Tea Party started. Follow the red line along Washington Street to Old State House (► 43). A circle of stones in the traffic island on State Street marks the site of the Boston Massacre. Cross onto Congress Street to get to Faneuil Hall (► 44).

The trail continues between the Holocaust Memorial (► 57) and the Olde Union Oyster House to Hanover Street. Cross Blackstone Street and follow the walkway under the Expressway to the North End. Turn onto Richmond Street to reach North Square and Paul Revere House (► 47). Back in Hanover Street, turn onto Revere Mall, passing Paul Revere's statue, with Old North Church (► 46) steeple ahead. Continue uphill to Copp's Hill Burying Ground (► 58).

INFORMATION

Distance 2.5km (1.5 miles)
Time 1–4 hours
Start point ★
Massachusetts State
House, Beacon Street
🔛 bIV; G4
🚇 Park
End point Copp's Hill
🔛 dI; H3
🚇 North Station

FOLLOW THE RED LINE

The Freedom Trail is a walking tour (self-guided or guided) that links the most significant sites from Boston's colonial and revolutionary era. A red line (made by paint or bricks) on the sidewalk makes it easy to follow. The Trail continues from Copp's Hill to Charlestown and USS *Constitution*.

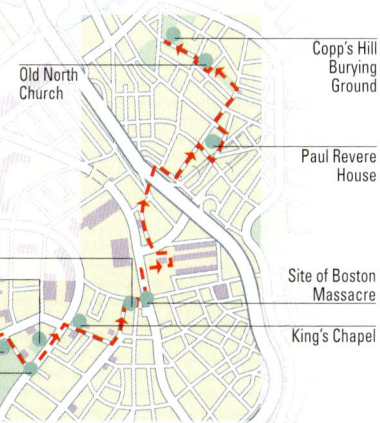

Copp's Hill Burying Ground

Old North Church

Paul Revere House

Old State House

Old Granary Burying Ground

State House

Shaw Monument

Site of Boston Massacre

King's Chapel

Brimstone Corner

Boston by Night

Above: *looking towards the Hancock Tower from the Prudential Tower*
Above right: *Fenway Park, home of the Red Sox*

LIVE ENTERTAINMENT

Listings in the *Boston Globe* range from the big-name Boston Symphony, Boston Ballet, and travelling Broadway shows to rock concerts, avant-garde dance, and radical student theatre. In summer, you can see free films, concerts, and theatre productions on outdoor stages. There are concerts throughout the summer at Hatch Shell (► 80), as well as free films on Fridays. Watch for free band concerts on City Hall Plaza (☎ 617/635–4505) in July and August, and for performances across the city by Boston Landmarks Orchestra (☎ 617/520–2200; www. landmarksorchestra. org).

ILLUMINATIONS

For magical views of Boston's skyline visit the Prudential Skywalk or cross over the Charles River to Cambridge on the T. Memorial Drive, between Longfellow and Harvard bridges, is also a good spot to view the floodlit downtown skyscrapers. In winter, Boston's trees twinkle with white lights.

PEOPLE-WATCHING

One of the liveliest spots for people-watching is the North End, where Italian music fills the narrow streets and restaurants hum with the chatter of Italian families. In Faneuil Hall, food vendors ply their trade in the floodlit open-air marketplace, while at Harvard Square street performers often share the sidewalks with strollers. In Newbury Street people sit outdoors in cafés surveying the pedestrian parade.

CLUBS AND BARS

Boston club kids head for Lansdowne Street, near Kenmore Square. To sip cocktails and catch the latest music, young professionals go to Boylston Place, a little alley in the Theater District. The Bull & Finch pub (► 71), which inspired the TV series Cheers, is a popular tourist attraction.

LATE-NIGHT RESTAURANTS

Most restaurants do not serve after 10PM. If you are eating late, you could try Chinatown, where many places stay open until 4AM, (although care should be taken here after midnight—the area borders the Combat Zone, the red-light district on lower Washington Street). In the South End, several restaurants serve until 1AM on weekends.

BOSTON's
top 25 sights

The sights are shown on the maps on the inside front cover and inside back cover, numbered **1**–**25** across the city

Longfellow House & Brattle Street

HIGHLIGHTS

- Longfellow's study
- Chair made from the "spreading chestnut tree"

DID YOU KNOW?

- Longfellow could speak 8 languages and read and write in 12

INFORMATION

- B2; locator map A1
- Longfellow House: 105 Brattle Street, Cambridge
- 617/876–4492; www.nps.gov/long
- Longfellow House: summer: Wed–Sun 10–4.30
- None
- Harvard, then pleasant walk (0.8km/0.5miles)
- Good
- Inexpensive
- Harvard Square and University (► 27), Harvard University Museums (► 28)
- House tours

The clapboard houses on Brattle Street in Cambridge are beautiful examples of colonial architecture. One of them, Longfellow House, was Washington's base in the Revolution and later home of one of America's best-loved poets.

Tory Row Brattle Street starts close to Harvard Square. In the pre-Revolutionary 1770s the land on either side was owned by loyalist families (Tories), forced to quit when the patriots took over the area in 1774. No. 42, Brattle House, home of one such Tory, was later lived in by feminist author Margaret Fuller. The Dexter Pratt House, No. 56, now a bakery (► 70), was the home of the blacksmith of Longfellow's poem *The Village Blacksmith*. The shingle-fronted Stoughton House, No. 90, was designed by H. H. Richardson, of Trinity Church fame (► 34).

Longfellow House No. 105, built in 1759 on an estate that extended down to the river, was George Washington's base during the siege of Boston, 1775–76. The widow of a later owner took in lodgers and thus, in 1837, came Henry Wadsworth Longfellow, the new Professor of Modern Languages at Harvard University. He later married Frances "Fanny" Appleton, whose wealthy mill-owning father bought the house for them. Happily married, they raised six children here, entertaining the intellectuals of the day. It was here that Longfellow wrote many of his poems, including the *Song of Hiawatha* and *Paul Revere's Ride*. Take the tour through the dining room, parlour, library, bedrooms, and, of course, Longfellow's study.

Top: *Longfellow House*
Above: *Henry Wadsworth Longfellow*

Harvard Square & Harvard University

One of the most significant strands in the fabric of Bostonian life is the academic scene. In Cambridge you can walk through hallowed Harvard Yard in the footsteps of the great, then enjoy the funky scene in Harvard Square.

Strolling through Harvard Square

Harvard University Among the first things the Massachusetts Bay colonists did was to provide for the training of ministers, and thus was founded, in 1636, what became one of the world's most respected seats of learning. Most of its historic buildings are in Harvard Yard, entered across the street from the First Parish Church. Ahead, in front of Bulfinch's granite University Hall is a statue by Daniel Chester French of benefactor John Harvard, famous for its "three lies" (Harvard was not the founder; a student, not Harvard, was the model; the foundation date is wrong). The elegant 18th-century redbrick halls grouped around this, the Old Yard, are dormitories. Behind University Hall is New Yard, with Memorial Church on the left facing the pillared facade of Widener Library. Groups of students move quietly across the grassy lawns. Pass beside H. H. Richardson's Sever Hall to emerge in Quincy Street opposite the Carpenter Center for the Visual Arts, the only Le Corbusier building in North America. The Fogg Art Museum (►28) is next door. Radcliffe Institute, formerly a women's college, is alongside Cambridge Common, around the lovely Radcliffe Yard.

Harvard Square The newsstand by the T is a famous landmark in this irregularly shaped "square." In and around it you can watch chess games, listen to street musicians, sit in an outdoor café, shop for trendy clothes, browse in bookshops, or go to a club for jazz or reggae.

HIGHLIGHTS

- Harvard Yard
- Radcliffe Yard
- Browsing in a bookshop all evening

INFORMATION

- ✚ C2; locator map B1
- ✉ Harvard University: Harvard Yard, Peabody Street, Cambridge
- ☎ Visitor Information Booth 617/497–1630; University 617/495–1573; www.harvard.edu
- 🕐 Daily
- 🍴 Plenty
- Ⓣ Harvard
- 💲 Free
- ↔ Longfellow House (►26), Harvard University Museums (►28)
- ❓ Campus tours Mon–Fri 10, 2; Sat 2

Harvard University Museums

HIGHLIGHTS

- Impressionists (Fogg)
- Jade (Sackler)
- Glass flowers (HMNH)

INFORMATION

✚ C2; locator map B1

✉ Fogg & Busch-Reisinger: 32 Quincy Street. Sackler: 485 Broadway. HMNH: 24 Oxford Street

☎ Art museums: 617/495–9400. HMNH: 617/495–3045; www.harvard.edu

◔ Art museums: Mon–Sat 10–5; Sun 1–5. HMNH: daily 9–5

♿ Very good

💵 Moderate. Art museums free Sat AM & Wed. HMNH free Sun AM, and Wed PM Sep–May. CityPass applies

Top: Fogg Art Museum
Below: The Crucifixion by Lorenzetti Ambrogio

Few universities have such an enviable collection. The pieces in Harvard's three art museums, each of which has its own character, are of a quality to rival any in the world.

Fogg Art Museum The galleries of the Fogg Art Museum are arranged around a Renaissance-style arcaded courtyard, a delightful setting for a remarkable collection of Western art. The Italian early Renaissance period is particularly well represented, with gems from artists such as Simone Martini, Bernardo Daddi, and Filippo Lippi. In other rooms find Dutch and Flemish paintings and a charming collection of Bernini clay models. Upstairs galleries feature major American landscape painters, an Impressionist collection with familiar pieces by all the major artists, and some important Picassos.

Busch-Reisinger Museum Reached through the upper floor of the Fogg, this small museum focuses on Expressionist art of Central and Northern Europe, with Bauhaus artefacts and paintings by Kandinsky, Klee, and Moholy-Nagy.

Arthur M. Sackler Museum Next door, the Sackler building is by British architect Sir James Stirling. Along with one of the best collections of Chinese jade in the world, it houses Chinese bronzes, Japanese prints, Indian art, and Greek and Roman vases and sculptures—all superb.

Harvard Museum of Natural History (HMNH) Here the Glass Flower exhibits make the short walk from the art museums well worth it. There are more than 3,000 models of 830 species of flowers and plants, some with insects, all so realistic you simply cannot believe they are made of glass.

Isabella Stewart Gardner Museum

The woman who created this collection of "beautiful things" had a passion for art, music, and horticulture. Her finds are arranged in a Venetian-style house built around a flower-filled courtyard.

"Beautiful things" Determined to give her "very young country" the opportunity of "seeing beautiful things," the much-travelled Mrs. Gardner made a start in 1896 by buying a Rembrandt self-portrait. Her collection grew to include work by artists such as Giotto, Botticelli, Raphael, Vermeer, Degas, and Matisse, as well as her friends John Singer Sargent and James McNeill Whistler. She also acquired prints and drawings, books, sculptures, ceramics and glass, carpets, tapestries, lace, stained glass, ironwork, and furniture.

Music and horticulture The building itself, known as Fenway Court, and the atmosphere that pervades it, is as much the creation of Mrs. Gardner as her collection. She arranged her objects in a series of rooms—the Raphael Room, the Titian Room, the Gothic Room, the intimate Blue Room, and more. She filled the courtyard with sculptures, plants, and trees, and she celebrated the opening of her home (she lived on the top floor) to the public with a concert given by members of the Boston Symphony Orchestra. Today, concerts are held in the Tapestry Room on winter weekends.

Art heist The collection suffered a terrible loss—and America's biggest art theft—in March 1990 when thieves dressed as policemen made off with 13 items. Among them were a priceless Vermeer and *The Sea of Galilee*, Rembrandt's only seascape. The pieces are still missing and, as Mrs. Gardner forbade any re-arrangement, the empty frames remain poignantly in place.

HIGHLIGHTS

- The courtyard, any season
- The personal feel of the collection
- Afternoon concerts on winter weekends

INFORMATION

- ⊞ D6; locator map A4
- ✉ 280 The Fenway, Back Bay
- ☎ 617/566–1401; www.gardnermuseum.org
- ◷ Tue–Sun 11–5. Closed Mon except most public hols
- 🍴 On premises
- 🚇 Museum (green line E)
- ♿ Good
- 🎫 Expensive. Boston CityPass applies
- ↔ Museum of Fine Arts (➤ 30)
- ❓ Concerts Sep–Apr: Sat, Sun 1.30
  ☎ 617/734–1359.
  Tour Fri 2.30.
  Courtyard talks most weekdays (times posted at the information desk). Lectures, shop

The courtyard—fountains, ferns, and fragrant flowering plants

29

Museum of Fine Arts

HIGHLIGHTS

- Nubian collection
- Impressionist room
- Copley portraits
- Tang dynasty earthenware

INFORMATION

- ✚ E6; locator map A4
- ✉ 465 Huntington Avenue
- ☎ 617/267–9300;
  www.mfa.org
- ◉ Mon, Tue 10–4.45;
  Wed–Fri 10–9.45 (Thu, Fri
  after 5, Evans Wing and
  selected galleries only);
  Sat, Sun 10–5.45
- 🍴 Choice on premises
- Ⓜ Museum (green line E)
- ♿ Excellent
- 💰 Expensive. Wed 4–9.45
  voluntary contribution.
  Boston CityPass applies
- ❓ Guided walks Mon–Sat.
  Tea and Music Tue–Fri
  2.30–4. Lectures, films,
  concerts. Good shop

Winslow Homer, Long
Branch, *detail*

The MFA is one of America's foremost museums. The Asian collection is unrivalled in this hemisphere, the European art is superb, the American rooms excellent. If time is limited, take a guided tour of the highlights.

Asian, Egyptian, classical The MFA's Nubian collection is the best outside the Sudan. It is all exquisite, from the neat rows of little *shawabtis* (figurines) to the faience jewellery. The Egyptian rooms are popular, with mummies, hieroglyphics, and splendid Old Kingdom sculptures. Buddhist sculptures, Chinese ceramics, and Indian paintings make up part of an Asian collection. Outside, take in the Japanese Tenshin Garden (spring to early autumn).

European In the Evans Wing upstairs, seek out the little gem of a Rembrandt in a glass case, then take in works of Tiepolo, Gainsborough, Turner, Delacroix, Constable, and a good number of Millets. The Impressionist room is an array of familiar paintings, from Monet and Renoir to Gauguin. There is porcelain from all over Europe and period rooms from Britain.

American New England furniture and decorative arts feature in a series of period rooms. Near the silver (note Paul Revere's work) is a fine musical instruments collection. As for the art of New England, downstairs in the Evans Wing, begin with the Copley portraits, work through the 19th-century landscape painters Bierstadt, Fitz Hugh Lane, and Thomas Cole, and move on to Winslow Homer and John Singer Sargent, and, from the 20th century, Childe Hassam, Edward Hopper, and Lilian Westacott Hale. In the Contemporary Art room find work by Georgia O'Keeffe and Stuart Davis.

First Church of Christ, Scientist

The scale of this complex is mind-blowing. The world headquarters for the Church of Christ, Scientist, occupies 14 acres of prime Back Bay land, with a church seating 3,000. The library houses the remarkable Mapparium.

World headquarters Perhaps the best place from which to appreciate the vast size of the complex is the top of the Prudential Tower (▶ 32). From here you look down on its 82m (270-ft) reflecting pool and the small granite original Mother Church with its huge domed basilica-type extension. At the far end of the pool is the Mary Baker Eddy Library, where the Mapparium is housed, while nearer the Pru is the office tower.

The churches The Mother Church of Christian Science was founded in Boston in 1892 by Mary Baker Eddy. The original church building was opened in 1894 but the numbers of believers in spiritual healing grew so rapidly that an extension was built in 1906, seating 3,000. The huge open space here is dominated by one of the world's largest organs, played at every service.

Mary Baker Eddy Library and the Mapparium The reference library holds all Eddy's writings, plus some 10,000 books on spirituality and healing. The Mapparium, on the first floor, is a brightly coloured stained-glass globe, so huge you can walk inside it and stand at the centre of the world. It shows the political boundaries of the early 1930s, when it was made. Try out the echo—sound waves bounce back off the glass, creating decidedly weird effects. The *Christian Science Monitor* exhibit features this highly respected international daily newspaper, founded by Eddy in 1908 and read by many outside the movement for its unbiased reporting.

Top: *Mapparium*
Above: *the Mother Church*

DID YOU KNOW?

- The Mapparium has 608 panels, each covering 10 degrees of latitude and longitude
- The Mary Baker Eddy Library is the largest single collection put together by an American woman

INFORMATION

- ✚ F6; locator map A4
- ✉ 175 Huntington Avenue
- ☎ 617/450–2000; 24-hour information 617/450–3709
- 🕐 Daily
- 🍴 Nearby in Prudential Center
- Ⓟ Prudential
- ♿ Good
- 💲 Free
- ↔ Prudential Skywalk (▶ 32)
- ❓ Tours of the Mother Church are available

Prudential Skywalk & Hancock Tower

The Hancock Tower, seen from the Pru

Two very different towers: one a 1970s landmark building to be admired from street level; the other architecturally unremarkable but offering bird's eye views of Boston and the New England countryside from its 50th floor.

John Hancock Tower There is something immensely serene about this icy shaft of blue glass thrusting upwards to join the clouds, no matter how ephemeral it looks beside Trinity Church, whose solid granite is reflected in its lowest windows. Designed by Henry Cobb, of I. M. Pei & Partners, in 1976 for the John Hancock Insurance Company, the building caused a big sensation at first, particularly when its panes of glass kept popping out and smashing on the street below. But it has long since found a place in (most) Bostonians' hearts. After the New York World Trade Center attacks on September 11, 2001, an observatory on the 60th floor was closed to the public, for security reasons.

Skywalk at the Prudential Tower By contrast, the nearby Prudential Tower is architecturally undistinguished, part of the 1960s Prudential Center office and shopping complex. But take the elevator to the Skywalk on the 50th floor and you have stunning 360-degree views—weather permitting, as far as the mountains of Vermont. Pick out the gold dome of the State House; peer down onto the rooftops of the neat Back Bay terraces and over the Charles River to MIT and Cambridge; see the parks of the Emerald Necklace (➤ 59) stretching into the distance; look out to the Boston Harbor Islands. Interactive exhibits fill you in on key historical and sporting events, as well as distinguished buildings and residents. On the 52nd floor is the Top of the Hub bar and restaurant.

Boston Public Library

This is no ordinary library. Behind its august granite facade lies an opulent institution built in the style of a Renaissance *palazzo* and decorated with sculptures and paintings by some of the greatest artists of the day.

The education of the people A people's palace dedicated to the advancement of learning was what Charles Follen McKim was commissioned to design. An architectural landmark in the classical style, facing H. H. Richardson's Romanesque Trinity Church across Copley Square, it opened its doors to the public in 1895. It is now the Research Library, the General Library being housed in the adjoining 1972 Johnson Building.

Further treasures Pass between Bela Pratt's voluptuous bronzes, *Science* and *Art* (1912), to enter through Daniel Chester French's bronze doors. Ascend the marble staircase, guarded by lions by Louis Saint-Gaudens (Augustus' brother), and from its windows catch a glimpse of the peaceful courtyard around which the library is built. The stairs and landing are decorated with panels by Puvis de Chavannes, whimsical representations of the muses of inspiration. The Abbey Room has paintings depicting the quest for the Holy Grail, by Edwin Austin Abbey. Bates Hall is a magnificent room; get a close-up view of its highly decorative, barrel-vaulted ceiling from the stairs that lead up to the Sargent Gallery. The John Singer Sargent murals, *Triumph of Religion*, completed in 1919, are undergoing phased restoration. Back downstairs, sit in the colonnaded courtyard for a while, watching the *Bacchante* fountain play and enjoying the tranquillity.

HIGHLIGHTS

- Puvis de Chavannes murals
- John Singer Sargent murals
- Daniel Chester French bronze doors
- The courtyard

INFORMATION

- F5; locator map B4
- Copley Square
- 617/536–5400; www.bpl.org
- Mon–Thu 9–9; Fri, Sat 9–5. Oct–May: Sun 1–5. Jun–Sep: closed Sun
- Nearby
- Copley
- Good
- Free
- Tours (Dartmouth Street entrance) Mon 2.30; Tue, Thu 6; Fri, Sat 11. Also Sun 2 (Oct–May only). Lectures

Top: *staircase*
Below: *courtyard*

Trinity Church

H. H. Richardson's prototype French Romanesque church is often described as America's masterpiece of ecclesiastical architecture. A greater contrast to the John Hancock Tower next door can hardly be imagined.

Top: *La Farge murals*
Above: *west front*

HIGHLIGHTS

- Polychrome interior
- John La Farge paintings and lancet windows
- Reflection in John Hancock Tower
- Christmas candlelight services

INFORMATION

- F5; locator map B3
- Copley Square
- 617/536–0944; www. trinitychurchboston.org
- Daily 8–6
- Nearby
- Copley
- Good
- Free
- Hancock Tower (➤ 32), Boston Public Library (➤ 33)
- Free half-hour organ recitals Fri 12.15. Sun services 8, 9, 11 (with choir music), 6

French origins The Back Bay was a newly developed landfill area when the Copley Square site was bought and Henry Hobson Richardson was commissioned, in 1872, to draw up designs for a new Trinity Church. Richardson based his lay-out on 11th-century Romanesque churches in the Auvergne, in France. A massive lantern tower over the transept crossing would dominate the church inside and out, requiring more than 2,000 wooden piles massed together to support its granite foundations. Externally, the chunky granite blocks are broken up by bands of pink sandstone.

The fine-arts interior Inside, John La Farge created an intricate polychrome interior, a tapestry of rich reds and greens highlighted with gold. The arches beneath the great tower are decorated with La Farge murals painted in 1876–77, and it was he who supervised the stained glass, some by Edward Burne-Jones and William Morris. La Farge's own small but vibrant, turquoise lancet windows are in the north transept, west wall. The decorated pipes of the organ in the west end are notable (music at Trinity is important—look out for concerts). In the baptistery is a bust by Daniel Chester French of the portly rector Phillips Brooks, whose greatest claim to fame is his carol "O Little Town of Bethlehem." His statue, by Augustus Saint-Gaudens, stands outside the north transept. At the east end there is a small cloister and garden.

Back Bay & Commonwealth Avenue

A Parisian-style boulevard lined with the grandest houses in Boston is at the heart of an amazing piece of 19th-century urban planning. To walk down it is to be transported to a different age.

Samuel Eliot Morison statue, Commonwealth Avenue

Landfill By the 1850s, Boston, still a small peninsula, was getting overcrowded. Desperate for land, developers turned to the swampy "back bay" of the Charles River, embarking on a remarkable landfill project to create a whole new residential district. Inspired by Paris' boulevard system, the architect Arthur Gilman planned a grid, eight blocks long and four blocks wide, with a long central mall. Block by block, the new houses went up and the wealthy moved in.

Commonwealth Avenue and Newbury Street The nouveau-riche industrialists who flocked to the Back Bay felt none of the Puritan restraints of the Proper Bostonians of Beacon Hill, and their rows of ostentatious brownstones are an exuberant blend of Victorian styles. The centrepiece is Commonwealth Avenue. Central gardens are lined with trees; in spring magnolias bloom in profusion. A string of statues includes slavery abolitionist William Lloyd Garrison and naval historian Samuel Eliot Morison. See which house you like best—almost every one has something worthy of note. Most are now apartments, some are offices. The château-like Burrage Mansion at Hereford Street stands out, with statuettes everywhere. To see inside a more average home, visit Gibson House Museum on Beacon Street (▶ 54). After strolling down Commonwealth Avenue, walk back along Newbury Street for some stylish window-shopping (▶ 72). Also look for the Newbury Street trompe l'oeil murals at the Boston Architectural Center and No. 354.

HIGHLIGHTS

- Houses and magnolias on Commonwealth Avenue
- Window-shopping in Newbury Street
- People-watching in the Newbury Street cafés

DID YOU KNOW?

- North–south streets are named alphabetically, Arlington to Hereford

INFORMATION

- ✚ F5–G5; locator map B3
- 🍴 Newbury and Boylston streets
- 🚇 Arlington, Copley, Hynes
- ↔ First Church of Christ, Scientist (▶ 31), Hancock Tower (▶ 32), Prudential Skywalk (▶ 32), Boston Public Library (▶ 33), Trinity Church (▶ 34), Public Garden (▶ 38)

Museum of Science

HIGHLIGHTS

- Lightning demo
- Virtual FishTank
- Natural Mysteries
- Mugar Omni Theater shows

INFORMATION

- G3; locator map C1
- Science Park
- 617/723–2500; www.mos.org
- 5 Jul–Labor Day: daily 9–7 (Fri 9–9). Labor Day–4th of Jul: daily 9–5 (Fri 9–9). Extended hours over school holidays
- Three on premises
- Science Park
- Excellent. Sight- and hearing-impaired facilities
- Expensive. Separate tickets for Planetarium, Laser Show, Omni Theater. Combination ticket discounts. Boston CityPass applies
- Good shop

This place buzzes and hums with excited children running around pressing buttons and peering into things. There are hundreds of interactive exhibits, as well as live presentations.

Science now The Museum of Science prides itself on being at the cutting edge of science education. The museum complex straddles the Charles River, with fine views of the Cambridge and Boston skylines.

"It's awesome" Don't miss the dramatic indoor lightning demos in the Theater of Electricity, where the world's largest Van de Graaff generator creates 2.5 million volts of electricity. Between shows, the Virtual Volleyball exhibit is popular. Close by, peer into the mouth of a T. Rex, modelled to reflect the latest paleontological theories. In the Virtual FishTank create a fish then see how it interacts with other creatures when you release it into the ocean. Other popular exhibits include the Natural Mysteries, where you learn about scientific classification from collections of skulls, animal tracks, shells, and more. Seeing is Deceiving explores both visual and auditory illusions, while in Science in the Park you can work out why a swing swings. There are also presentations at the Science Live! Stage.

Mugar Omni, Planetarium, and Lasers Lie back and be totally enveloped in the sight and sound of an IMAX film in the five-storey domed screen of the Mugar Omni Theater. Multi-media presentations at the Planetarium cover various astronomical subjects, and there are evening laser shows.

Beacon Hill & Louisburg Square

Beacon Hill is an enclave of elegant redbrick houses in a leafy maze of steep streets and narrow, cobbled lanes—it is a delightful area to explore on foot.

Brahmin stronghold After the opening of the new State House on its southern slope, Beacon Hill was developed as a prestigious residential district by a group of entrepreneurs that included architect Charles Bulfinch (►11). Boston's top families swiftly moved in. Rich as they were, these Brahmins (►14) were also the personification of Puritan reserve. Showiness was taboo, so their new houses were the epitome of restraint, with elegant doorways and delicate ironwork gracing plain brick facades.

Perfectly preserved To get the magic of it all, choose a sunny day and just wander, noting the pillared porticoes, genteel fanlights, and flowery window boxes. The Beacon Hill walk (►22) leads you to some of the most treasured corners, including Mt. Vernon Street, Chestnut Street, tiny Acorn Street, and, best of all, Louisburg Square. Here Bulfinch's lovely bow fronts look onto a central garden reminiscent of a European square. Notice how the street lamps are lit all day and, in Beacon Street, look for the purple panes: Manganese oxide in a batch of glass reacted with sunlight to produce discoloured but, now, highly prized and very distinctive panes. To see inside a Beacon Hill home, visit the Nichols House Museum (►55). On the hill's north slope from Pinckney Street down to Cambridge Street, the houses are smaller and more varied in style, the overall effect less grand. It has several important sites in the history of Boston's African-American community, including the African Meeting House (►55).

HIGHLIGHTS

- Louisburg Square
- Pinckney Street and its view of Charles River
- Purple panes of glass, Beacon Street
- Charles Street shops and restaurants

INFORMATION

- ✚ a–blll–IV; G4; locator map C2
- ✉ Bounded by Beacon Street, Embankment Road, Cambridge Street, Bowdoin Street
- 🍴 Choice in Charles Street
- Ⓟ Park, Charles, Arlington, Bowdoin (closed Sat)
- ♿ Steep hills, some uneven surfaces
- ↔ Boston Common & the Public Garden (►38), Harrison Gray Otis House (►39), Massachusetts State House (►40), Boston Athenaeum (►41)
- ❓ SPNEA tours of Beacon Hill (►39), Black Heritage Trail: See Museum of Afro-American History (►55)

Boston Common & the Public Garden

Top: *Swan Boats,
Public Garden*
Above: *Boston Common*

DID YOU KNOW?

● The original Swan Boats
were inspired by
Wagner's *Lohengrin*

INFORMATION

✚ aIV–bIV; G5;
locator map C3

✉ Bounded by Beacon,
Park, Tremont, Boylston,
Arlington streets

☎ Swan Boats: 617/522–
1966. Ice-skating:
617/635-2120

🕐 Public Garden: daily
dawn–10PM.
Swan Boats: Apr–Sep.
Ice-skating: Nov–Mar

🍴 Nearby

Ⓣ Park, Boylston, Arlington

♿ Garden and Common
free. Swan Boats, skating
inexpensive

↔ Beacon Hill (► 37),
Massachusetts State
House (► 40), Boston
Athenaeum (► 41)

**Very different in history and character,
these adjoining pieces of public open
space, separated by Charles Street,
right in the heart of the city, are held in
deep affection. Without them, Boston
just wouldn't be Boston.**

Boston Common The oldest public park in the
US owes its origins to early British settlers who in
1634 acquired the land from a Reverend William
Blaxton for common grazing. Being common
land, it was also where criminals were hanged,
witches were dunked, and the dead were buried
(in the Central Burying Ground, by Boylston
Street). Here, British soldiers camped and
George Washington addressed the crowds after
Independence. Early in the 1800s the gallows
were removed, cattle were banned, paths were
laid out, and fountains and monuments erected.
It is still a place for speeches and demonstrations,
but also for sport, for paddling, or, in winter, ice-
skating at Frog Pond, chasing the pigeons, eating
ice cream, listening to street performers and
concerts—and people-watching. Safe by day, it's
best avoided at night.

The Public Garden Much more genteel and
decorative, this was created as a botanical garden
in 1837 from reclaimed marshland. Hundreds of
trees were planted, and beds, lawns, and a lacing
of footpaths were laid out. The garden is
perennially beautiful and often fairytale-like.
The focal point is a pond, with a pretty little cast-
iron suspension bridge (the world's smallest).
Here, in summer, you can ride the famous Swan
Boats. Sculptures include a striking equestrian
George Washington (Thomas Ball, 1869), the Ether
Monument, marking the first use of ether as an
anaesthetic, here in Boston, in 1846, and *Make
Way for Ducklings* (► 61).

Harrison Gray Otis House

This is Boston's only remaining Federal-style mansion. Meticulously restored in its every detail, the gracious interior is an accurate representation of how the upper classes lived in the 19th century.

Otis and Bulfinch One of the leading lights in post-Revolutionary Boston politics was the lawyer Harrison Gray Otis (1765–1844), long-standing friend of architect Charles Bulfinch. A wealthy man moving in the upper echelons of Bostonian society, in 1796 he commissioned Bulfinch to build him this grand mansion in what was then the elegant area of Bowdoin Square. The structure's very restrained, very proper, brick facade is typical of what became known as the Federal style. Five years later, Bulfinch built Otis an even bigger house on newly developed Beacon Hill (▶ 37), to which all the wealthy were rapidly migrating. By the 1830s the Otis home had become a boarding house. Now the Otis House and the Old West Church next door are a little oasis of elegance in an area of less-than-lovely urban renewal.

Authenticity In 1916 the Society for the Preservation of New England Antiquities bought the property as its headquarters. Accuracy and authenticity being its hallmarks, the SPNEA has restored the interior with reproduction wallpapers and paint colours (some surprisingly bright) based on paint analysis. Otis and his wife, Sally, were lavish entertainers and the parlour, dining room, and drawing room, furnished in high Federal style, provide an insight into social manners of the day, while bedrooms, kitchens, and servant quarters give you a glimpse of family life. One upstairs room shows the mansion when it was a boarding house.

HIGHLIGHTS

- Bulfinch Federal design
- Reproductions of original wallpaper
- Yellow and turquoise paints
- Federal era furniture

DID YOU KNOW?

- In 1926 the house was moved back 12m (40 feet) because of road widening

INFORMATION

- ⊞ blll; G4; locator map D2
- ⊠ 141 Cambridge Street
- ☎ 617/227–3956; www.spnea.org
- 🕐 Wed–Sun 11–5. Tours on the hour. Last tour at 4
- 🍴 None
- 🚇 Bowdoin (closed Sat), Charles, Government Center
- ♿ Wheelchairs first floor only
- 💰 Moderate. SPNEA members free
- ↔ Beacon Hill (▶ 37), Massachusetts State House (▶ 40), Boston Athenaeum (▶ 41)
- ❓ Walking tours of Beacon Hill mid-May to mid-Oct, Sat (call ahead). Shop

Massachusetts State House

HIGHLIGHTS

- Gold dome (reguilded in 1997 with 22 carat gold leaf)
- Sacred Cod
- Senate Reception Room
- Senate Chamber

DID YOU KNOW?

- In 1858 Oliver Wendell Holmes called the State House the "hub of the solar system," a phrase expanded to "the universe" and applied to Boston as a whole
- Road distances out of Boston are measured from the dome

INFORMATION

- ✠ blll–blV; G4; locator map D2
- ✉ Beacon Street
- ☎ 617/727–3676
- 🕐 Mon–Fri 10–4 (except hol Mons)
- 🍴 None
- 🅿 Park
- ♿ Partial wheelchair access
- 🎟 Free
- ↔ Harrison Gray Otis House (➤ 39), Beacon Hill (➤ 37), Boston Athenaeum (➤ 41)
- ❓ Regular tours (45 minutes); last tour 3.30

Prosperous and newly independent in the late 18th century, Massachusetts needed a larger, more imposing State House. Charles Bulfinch's masterpiece is a landmark in American architecture.

Hub of the Hub Bulfinch began designing the new State House on his return from England, much influenced by Robert Adam's Renaissance style. Construction began in 1795 on a prominent piece of Beacon Hill land purchased from the estate of the wealthy merchant and patriot John Hancock. Cut off in your mind's eye the side wings (an early 20th-century addition), and focus on Bulfinch's dignified two-storey portico and the glistening dome. Its original shingles were covered in copper from the foundry of Paul Revere when the roof began to leak, and the gold leaf was added in 1874. Until skyscrapers arrived, it dominated the city skyline.

Seat of government Start your tour in the columned Doric Hall (the central door is for visiting presidents and retiring governors only). From here pass through the marble Nurses' Hall and note Bela Pratt's memorial to Civil War nurses. The Italian marble floor in the Hall of Flags was laid by immigrants from Italy living in the North End. Featured in the stained-glass skylight are the seals of the original 13 states. Up the staircase is the House of Representatives chamber. Here, the Sacred Cod, a symbol of the importance of the fishing industry and a lucky mascot, must hang whenever the 160 state representatives are in session. The dignified barrel-vaulted and Ionic-columned Senate Reception Room is Bulfinch's, as is the Senate Chamber, where 40 senators debate beneath a graceful sunburst dome. A larger-than-life *J.F.K.* (Isabel McIlvain, 1988) is one of several statues outside.

Boston Athenaeum

Many Bostonians have never been here. You must see what they are missing. Leave 21st-century hassle behind and enter what Henry James called "the haunt of all the most civilized."

Temple of Culture When the Athenaeum library moved to 10½ Beacon Street in 1849 it had been the centre of intellectual and cultural life in Boston for more than 40 years. Indeed, the paintings and sculptures it had accumulated formed the core of the Museum of Fine Arts' founding collection. Founded in 1807 to foster scholarship, literature, science, and the visual arts, it remains the haunt of Boston's intellectual elite. Several years of refurbishment and extensions have restored the building to its former glory and brought its facilities into the 21st century, while retaining the atmosphere of a less frenzied era. The collection of 600,000 volumes includes George Washington's personal library.

Silence Visitors have access to the first floor at any time and to other floors by guided tour (highly recommended; pre-booking is essential). Many of the library's important paintings hang in a large first-floor gallery. Glass walls screen a newspaper and magazine reading room. A splendid old elevator (now complemented by a modern one) takes members up to the glorious second-floor reading room and print room, a third-floor room where members may browse and converse quietly, and—the ultimate haven—a silent fifth-floor research room with a fine ceiling. On all floors long windows overlook the Old Granary Burying Ground, leather-upholstered chairs are drawn up to antique tables, oriental rugs cover the floors, books line the walls, busts and statues stand on plinths. There are fresh flowers in every room.

HIGHLIGHTS

- The civilized, unhurried atmosphere
- The reading rooms
- Paintings and sculptures
- Views of Old Granary Burying Ground

DID YOU KNOW?

- Afternoon tea is served to members on Wednesdays
- The fresh flowers are funded by a gift honouring a former member

INFORMATION

- ➕ clV; G4–G5; locator map D2–3
- ✉ 10½ Beacon Street
- ☎ 617/227–0270; www.bostonathenaeum.org
- 🕐 First floor: Mon 9–8; Tue–Fri 9–5.30. Also Sep–May Sat 9–4. Other floors: by tour only, Tue, Thu 3PM (you must book ahead)
- 🍴 Nearby
- 🌳 Park
- ♿ Wheelchair access
- 🆓 Free
- ↔ Beacon Hill (► 37), Massachusetts State House (► 40)
- ❓ Lectures, concerts

Old South Meeting House

What started life in 1729 as a Puritan meeting house was later, by reason only of its size, to witness one of the most significant moments in American history.

HIGHLIGHTS

- Plain Puritan interior
- Vial of tea from the Tea Party
- First book published by an African American

INFORMATION

- ✚ clV; H4; locator map E3
- ✉ Washington Street at Milk Street
- ☎ 617/482–6439; www.old southmeetinghouse.org
- ⊙ Apr–Oct: daily 9.30–5. Nov–Mar: daily 10–5
- 🍴 Nearby
- Ⓜ State, Downtown Crossing
- ♿ Good
- 💲 Inexpensive
- ↔ Old State House (➤ 43)
- ❓ Concerts, lectures, tours

Portrait of early settler etched onto glass

Sanctuary of freedom When things started to heat up in the years leading up to the Revolution, the town hall, Faneuil Hall, could no longer hold the crowds that were turning up, so this, the most spacious meeting place in the city, became their venue. Here the sparks of insurrection fanned by such speakers as Samuel Adams, James Otis, and John Hancock, ignited on the evening of 16 December 1773. For it was here that night that Adams famously declared "Gentlemen, this meeting can do nothing more to save the country"—the signal for a band of men disguised as Mohawk Indians to lead the people off to Boston Harbor and the so-called Boston Tea Party (➤ 16).

Under Threat In the siege of Boston that followed, British troops occupied Old South, ripping out the pews and using it as a riding school for the cavalry. After the Revolution, it was restored as a church, but in 1872 was replaced by the New Old South Church, located on the corner of Copley Square. Threatened with demolition, Old South was saved for its historical associations and has been a museum ever since. The plain white-painted pews and pulpit of this simple brick church are reproductions, but the two-tiered gallery is original. Visual displays tell the story of Old South and audios of fiery debates describe the whole Tea Party event in graphic detail.

Old State House

This is the city's oldest public building, once the seat of British colonial government. Surrounded by taller—but far less significant—buildings, it seems so tiny now. It holds a first-rate museum.

Colonial capitol Built in 1713 to replace an earlier Town House, the Old State House was the British governor's seat of office, home to the judicial court and to the Massachusetts Assembly. As such it was the scene of many a confrontation between the colonists and their rulers. It was here that James Otis railed against the "tyranny of taxation without representation" and it was under the balcony at the east end that the "Boston Massacre" took place in 1770: Five colonists were killed in a clash with British soldiers, a key event in the years leading up to the Revolution. From the same balcony, the Declaration of Independence was read on 18 July 1776, and is still read every 4th of July. At this point the gilded lion and unicorn on the east front, symbols of the British Crown, were destroyed. From 1780 until Bulfinch's new State House was opened on Beacon Hill in 1798, this was the Massachusetts State House. For most of the 19th century it was used for commercial purposes, gradually falling into disrepair until the Bostonian Society was founded in 1881 to restore it. The lion and unicorn were returned to their place, balanced now by the American eagle and the Massachusetts seal on the west end.

A museum of Boston The building is now home to the Bostonian Society's excellent museum. It traces the city's topographical, political, economic, and social history with a fine collection of maritime art, revolutionary memorabilia, prints, domestic objects, and audio exhibits.

HIGHLIGHTS

- Lion and unicorn
- Balcony from which the Declaration of Independence was read
- Exhibit showing typographical changes

INFORMATION

- ✚ c–dlll; H4; locator map E2
- ✉ 206 Washington Street
- ☎ 617/720–3289
- 🕐 Daily 9–5
- 🍴 Nearby
- Ⓡ State
- ♿ No access to upper floor
- 💲 Inexpensive
- ↔ Old South Meeting House (► 42), Faneuil Hall (► 44)
- ❓ Shop

Faneuil Hall & Marketplace

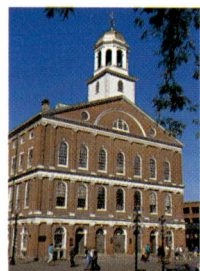

Faneuil Hall

Faneuil Hall is a landmark for all Americans, the place where the iniquities of the British government were first debated in the 1770s. Now, its marketplace is a landmark for visitors of every nation—as well as Bostonians.

HIGHLIGHTS

- Bulfinch meeting room
- Grasshopper weathervane on the roof
- Quincy's granite market buildings
- Street entertainers

INFORMATION

- dlll; H4; locator map E2
- Congress Street
- 617/242–5642; www. faneuilhallmarketplace. com
- Great Hall: 9–5 (when not in use)
- A plethora of eating places
- State, Aquarium, Government Center
- Good
- Great Hall: free
- Old State House (► 43)
- Great Hall: 15-minute talk every half-hour

The Cradle of Liberty A wealthy trader of Huguenot origins, Peter Faneuil (pronounced either "Fannel" or to rhyme with Daniel), presented the town with a market hall with a meeting room above. Ever since, the lower hall has been a market, and the galleried upper hall has been a place for public gatherings. In the 1700s, because the town meetings frequently discussed the problems with Britain that led up to the revolution and independence, Faneuil Hall became known as America's Cradle of Liberty. Since then national issues from the abolition of slavery to the Vietnam War have been aired here. If the Great Hall is not in use, go in to hear the guide's account of the Revolution. The room bears all the trademarks of Charles Bulfinch (► 11), who expanded it in 1805.

Quincy's marketplace The Bulfinch expansion soon proved to be inadequate as more space was needed. In 1826, with an inspired piece of town planning that radically changed Boston's waterfront, mayor Josiah Quincy filled in Town Dock and built over the wharves, providing a granite market hall flanked by granite warehouses. These were a wholesale food market until the 1960s. In the 1970s the area was renovated and revitalized, and is now the city's main tourist attraction (known as either Faneuil Hall Marketplace or Quincy Market) with dozens of shops, pushcarts, stands, eating places, and street entertainers. The Durgin Park dining rooms are an institution (► 64).

USS *Constitution* & Charlestown

"Old Ironsides," as she is widely known by schoolchildren, is the oldest commissioned warship afloat in the world. Over 200 years old, she is moored across the Charles River in the Charlestown Navy Yard.

The Navy Yard From 1800 to 1974 the Charlestown Navy Yard played an important role building, repairing, and supplying Navy warships. Its mission now is to interpret the history of naval shipbuilding. Representing the ships built here are USS *Constitution* and the World War II destroyer USS *Cassin Young*, both of which may be boarded. The old granite Building 22 now houses the USS *Constitution* Museum, where journals and maritime objects record the frigate's 200-year career in both war and peace and give a picture of life aboard. Also open is the Commandant's House. The Bunker Hill Pavilion's multi-media show, "Whites of Their Eyes," tells the story of the Battle of Bunker Hill, which actually took place nearby on Breed's Hill, on which stands the Bunker Hill Monument. This obelisk is visible from and within walking distance of the yard. Climb its 294 steps for good views.

USS *Constitution* The highlight of the Navy Yard is "Old Ironsides." Launched in Boston in 1797, she is still part of the US Navy, whose sailors lead tours round the cramped quarters and stand proudly by the neat coils of rope, glistening brass, and rows of guns. Vulnerable though the wooden sides seem now, it was her tough live-oak frames that enabled her to survive the War of 1812 undefeated and win her her nickname. A frail old lady, heavily reconstructed, she takes a turn in Boston Harbor every year on the 4th of July, changing the side that faces the elements.

HIGHLIGHTS

- Museum: details of a sailor's daily diet and duties
- USS *Constitution*: cramped lower deck

INFORMATION

- ✚ H3; locator map E1
- ✉ Charlestown Navy Yard
- ☎ Navy Yard Visitor Center: 617/242–5601; www.uss constitutionmuseum.org. "Whites of Their Eyes" reservations: 617/241–7575
- 🕐 USS *Constitution*: daily 10–4.
  USS *Cassin Young*: daily 10–4.
  Bunker Hill Monument: daily 9–4.30.
  Base Lodge (toy soldier battle display): daily 9–5.
  Museum: May–Oct: daily 9–6. Nov–Apr: daily 10–5.
  Bunker Hill Pavilion "White of Their Eyes": Apr–Nov daily 9.30–4
- 🍴 In the Yard
- Ⓡ North Station or Community College, then 15-minute walk
- 🚢 MBTA Water Shuttle from Long Wharf
- ♿ All wheelchair accessible except USS *Cassin Young*
- 🎟 All free except "Whites of Their Eyes" (inexpensive)
- ❓ Summer tours of Navy Yard (11AM).
  Museum shop

45

The North End & Old North Church

HIGHLIGHTS

- Paul Revere House
  (➤ 47)
- Old North Church Steeple
- Copp's Hill Burying
  Ground (➤ 58)
- Feast day processions
- Italian groceries, coffee
  shops, and restaurants

INFORMATION

- ✛ d–cl–ll; H3–H4;
  locator map E1
- ✉ Bounded by Commercial
  Street and Expressway
- ◷ Old North Church: all
  year (steeple: Jun–Oct)
- 🍽 Plenty around Hanover
  and Salem streets
- 🚇 Haymarket, North Station,
  Aquarium, State
- ♿ Some hills

The North End is Boston's oldest and most spirited district. This is where the British colonists settled in the 17th century, and now, after various ups and downs, it is a lively Italian quarter.

Little Italy The North End is separated from the rest of Boston by the J.F.K. Expressway (while work on putting it below ground continues, take the walkway underneath). When the colonists arrived it was also all but cut off, surrounded then by water at the end of a narrow peninsula. The colonists' erratic street plan survives, but the only building from the 17th century is Paul Revere House (➤ 47). Once the elite had moved to Beacon Hill in the early 19th century, the area played host to waves of immigrants, first the Irish, then East European and Portuguese, and finally Italians. It is the Italians who have given the area its current flavour, with Italian spoken in the streets, Italian music playing in the cafés, and lively street festivals (*festa*) in July and August.

Old North Church St. Stephen's Church (the only Bulfinch-designed church still standing in Boston) in the main artery of Hanover Street faces Revere's statue (➤ 57) and, behind it, the tall white steeple of Old North Church. It was from Old North that Revere's signal was given to the patriots in Charlestown that the British were on their way to Lexington where, the next day, the first battle of the War of Independence took place. Up the hill from Old North is Copp's Hill Burying Ground (➤ 58). From here wind down Snowhill and through the tall, narrow streets to Salem Street and, perhaps, a treat from a *pasticceria*.

*Old North
steeple*

Paul Revere House

This house is all that remains of the 17th-century settlement in today's North End. Not only is it Boston's oldest building, it was home to its most celebrated son, Paul Revere.

The early years The steep-gabled clapboard house that we see today was built in about 1680. Like most houses of the period, it had two rooms on each of its two floors but the positioning of the main staircase at the side of the building, making the rooms larger than normal, was unusual. By 1770, when the silversmith and engraver Paul Revere (▶ 17) came to live here, a number of significant alterations had been made, notably the addition of a third floor and a two-storey extension at the back. The family lived here during the Revolution, so it was from here that Revere set out on that famous midnight ride. In 1800, after the family sold the house, it became a rooming house, with shops and factory premises on the lower floor. Threatened with demolition in 1902, it was saved by Revere's great-grandson and, restored to something like its origins, became a museum.

The house today The basic timber skeleton of the house is the original, but the exterior clapboarding, the windows, and most of what you see inside are replacements. Go through the kitchen into the living room, furnished in period style. Upstairs, the main bedroom is an elegantly furnished room, which would have doubled as a parlour. In the other room, note the ingenious folding bed and its traditional woven cover.

HIGHLIGHTS

- Revere's own account of his ride
- Period furnishings

INFORMATION

- dll; H4; locator map E2
- 19 North Square
- 617/523–2338; www.paul reverehouse.org
- Nov to mid-Apr: daily 9.30–4.15. Mid-Apr to Oct: daily 9.30–5.15. Jan–Mar: closed Mon
- Nearby
- Government Center, State, Aquarium, Haymarket
- Wheelchair access first floor only
- Inexpensive
- Tours of early Georgian Pierce/Hichborn House

Bronze bell cast by Paul Revere

New England Aquarium

HIGHLIGHTS

- Giant Ocean Tank
- Medical Center
- The huge green sea turtle
- Little Blue penguins
- Whale-watching trip
- IMAX 3D films

INFORMATION

- elll; J4; locator map F2
- Central Wharf
- 617/973–5200; www.neaq.org
- 1 Jul–Labor Day: Mon, Tue, Fri 9–6; Wed, Thu 9–8; Sat, Sun, hols 9–7. Rest of year: Mon–Fri 9–5; Sat, Sun, hols 9–6
- On premises
- Aquarium
- Good
- Expensive (IMAX is extra). Boston CityPass applies
- Whale-watching Apr–Oct 617/973–5281. Shop

One of the largest aquatic collections in the world, this is a popular family excursion. A spiral ramp leads you around a vast cylindrical tank swirling with sea creatures of every imaginable size, shape, and colour.

Penguins, sharks, and electric eels In the penguin pool at the base of the Giant Ocean Tank pick out the world's smallest species, the Little Blues, then head left, past the Medical Center. Either go outside for a sea lion presentation or turn right, up the straight ramp, to the Thinking Gallery, where you can compare your hearing to that of a dolphin and your skeleton to that of a fish. The Freshwater Gallery has above- and below-surface views of a flooded Amazon forest complete with anaconda, alongside, by contrast, a New England trout stream. Don't miss the electric eel. Eventually, you reach the top of the huge tank at the heart of the Aquarium. At feeding times, approximately hourly, staff dive in, scattering squid for the bigger fish, jamming lettuce into the fibreglass coral reef for the angel fish, hand-feeding the sharks, and giving the turtles their vitamin-enriched gelatin (to keep their shells hard). Notice how all the fish swim in the same direction, into the current set up by the filter, to get more oxygen.

From big screen to deep waters To experience places that cannot be re-created in the aquarium, watch one of the aquatic films showing at the IMAX theatre. Alternatively, take the excellent *Voyager III* whale-watching trip.

Boston Harbor Islands

Gather wild raspberries, picnic on a beach, visit a ruined fort—all within sight of the city? These wildernesses are ringed by Boston, its airport, and suburbs: It's just incredible they've escaped development.

America's newest national park Having played their part in history as defensive sites and home to prisons and poorhouses, the Boston Harbor Islands were largely ignored until they became a National Recreation Area in 1996. People are only now beginning to appreciate these havens of wildlife, so near, yet so distant in feel.

Island hopping It's a 45-minute ferry ride from Long Wharf to Georges Island. From here water taxis loop to Lovells, Peddocks, Bumpkin, and Grape. The islands are small, so you can visit more than one in a day; each has its own character. Georges attracts most visitors; on the others you may be all alone. All have picnic areas (bring a picnic as there's no fresh water). Take guided walks, hike trails on your own, or just beachcomb (beaches are mostly pebbly). Lovells has a sandy, supervised swimming beach.

Something for everyone On Georges clamber over Fort Warren, where Civil War soldiers were imprisoned (find the hidden spiral staircase and get superb views of the city skyline). Peddocks and Lovells also have ruined forts. Bumpkin is where to pick raspberries. Join the hares on Lovells; study the wildlife in the rock pools, salt marsh, and woodland on Peddocks; and on Grape, crunch along beaches covered in iridescent blue mussel shells. All the islands are good for bird-watching. Little Brewster is home to the Boston Light (group tours only), the oldest lighthouse in the US and the only one still manned.

HIGHLIGHTS

- The sense of escape
- Picnicking on a beach
- Fort Warren's dungeons
- Views of Boston's skyline

INFORMATION

- ✚ Off map;
  off locator map at F2
- ✉ Boston Harbor Islands, National Park Service, 408 Atlantic Avenue, Boston, MA 02210-3350
- ☎ 617/223–8666; www.nps.gov/boha
- 🕐 Georges Island: May to mid-Oct, daily ferries (☎ 617/227–4321). The other islands: mid-Jun to Labor Day, daily. Labor Day to mid-Oct, Sat, Sun. May to mid-June, Sat, Sun
- 🍴 Snack bar and barbecues on Georges. No drinking water on any islands. Take a picnic
- 🛳 Long Wharf to Georges Island. Water taxis from Georges to four other islands (▶ above)
- ♿ Difficult
- 💲 Ferry expensive. Water taxi free
- ❓ Organized activities and tours. For lighthouse and occasional winter trips ☎ 781/740–4299

Wooded Grape Island, with Boston's suburban skyline beyond

John F. Kennedy Library & Museum

"A man may die, nations may rise and fall, but an idea lives on," said the late president John F. Kennedy, whose life, leadership, and legacy are brilliantly evoked in this dramatic museum by the sea.

The setting The presidential library and its museum, constructed in 1979, are housed in an I. M. Pei building on Dorchester Bay, 6.5km (4 miles) southeast of downtown Boston. The building's two towers, of dark glass and smooth white concrete, command fine views of the city, the bay, and Boston Harbor Islands. The lawns, dune grass, and wild roses on the grounds recall the Kennedy summer home on Cape Cod.

The New Museum An introductory film covers Kennedy's early years, from his childhood to the 1960 presidential campaign. Re-created settings include the White House corridors and the Oval Office, complete with the rocking chair J.F.K. used for his bad back and, on his desk, the coconut inscribed "HELP" that led to his rescue after his naval ship sank in the Pacific. Videos cover significant events such as the Cuban Missile Crisis, space exploration, and the assassination. There are family photographs and exhibits covering the life and work of First Lady Jacqueline Bouvier Kennedy.

The Presidential Library This is one of ten presidential libraries holding the papers of ten of the US presidents since Herbert Hoover. The Presidential Library System allows presidents to establish a library and museum wherever they choose. The J.F.K. Library is near his mother's home.

BOSTON's
best

Neighbourhoods

Harvard Square, Cambridge

CAMBRIDGE

Cambridge is a city with its own character on the other side of the Charles River, but it is so accessible it feels like part of Boston. Home to Harvard, MIT, and students from all around the world, Cambridge is nothing if not vibrant. There is lots to see and do in and around Harvard Square (► 27, 28), both by day and by night. Inman Square, Central Square, and Porter Square all have a diversity of international restaurants. By the river, MIT's campus boasts distinguished modern buildings and sculptures (► 56, 57). Farther north, there are good places to eat around Somerville's Davis Square and Union Square.

CHINATOWN AND THE THEATER DISTRICT

Bounded by Washington Street, Essex Street, Kneeland Street, and the Central Artery, between the Theater District and Financial District, Boston's Chinatown is not large but offers a real taste of Chinese daily life. The principal artery is Beach Street, with the traditional gateway at the eastern end. With the Theater District on the other side of Washington Street, Chinatown is handy for late eating. Its many restaurants offer Japanese, Vietnamese, and Korean cuisine, as well as Chinese. Be aware that the area borders the Combat Zone—the (rapidly shrinking) red-light district along lower Washington Street.

DOWNTOWN AND THE FINANCIAL DISTRICT

East of Boston Common is a mostly pedestrians-only shopping area, Downtown Crossing, that encompasses part of Washington Street and the streets that link it to Tremont Street. Department stores Filene's and Macy's are here, as well as Filene's Basement (► 74). The high-rise Financial District has some interesting art deco and modern buildings (► 56). Between here and Chinatown, cornered by Kneeland Street and Atlantic Avenue, the Leather District is a piece of 19th-century industrial Boston, whose redbrick buildings once serviced the shoe industry and now house offices, wine bars, and a gallery or two.

FENWAY AND KENMORE SQUARE

Art and sport meet here with the Museum of Fine Arts (► 30) and the Isabella Stewart Gardner Museum (► 29) on one side of the Back Bay Fens, and Fenway Park, home of the Red Sox, on the other. Boston University lies alongside the Charles River.

THE OLD WEST END, GOVERNMENT CENTER, AND FANEUIL HALL MARKETPLACE

The old West End is not an exciting district, but has the FleetCenter, home to the Celtics and Bruins (► 60), next to North Station. Beside the Charles River lies the granite Old Jail and hidden in Massachusetts General Hospital is the Ether Dome, where ether was first used as an anaesthetic. Nearby, Cambridge Street, at the northern foot of Beacon Hill, runs east to Government Center and City Hall Plaza, an impersonal area of office blocks facing Faneuil Hall and its lively Marketplace.

THE SOUTH END

First occupied by musicians and teachers in the 1850s, the South End had taken a social nose-dive by the end of the 19th century but is now very much back in vogue with young professionals and artists. It is a lively residential area, whose elegant bow-fronted terraces, many profusely decorated with balustrades and window boxes, line leafy streets and squares. Running through the middle is Tremont Street, where local shops are punctuated by trendy places to eat. There is a broad ethnic mix here and a strong gay element. The South End has a growing number of art galleries, particularly around Harrison and Thayer streets. The neighbourhood lies between Huntington Avenue and the Expressway.

WATERFRONT

The Waterfront, east of Faneuil Hall Marketplace, the North End, and the Financial District, will be changed beyond recognition once the Central Artery is finally buried and covered with a park (► 12). The old granite wharf buildings that once bustled with commercial activity are now luxury condos or offices overlooking trendy yacht havens. Boat trips leave from Long Wharf, the Aquarium (► 48), and Rowes Wharf. Across Fort Point Channel are Museum Wharf (► 61 for Children's Museum), the World Trade Center, and several seafood restaurants (► 66).

Ironwork typical of the South End

A SOUTH END STROLL

From Copley or Back Bay T, walk south down Dartmouth Avenue, over Columbus Avenue. Zigzag through Lawrence, Appleton, and Gray streets. Take Clarendon Street down to Tremont Street. Go right and left into Union Park. Go right (west) along Shawmut Avenue, right onto Upton or Pembroke Street. Turn left at Tremont, then right onto Rutland or Concord Square. Cut back across Columbus Avenue and up West Newton Street to Huntington Avenue and the Pru T.

53

Houses, Museums & Galleries

BROOKLINE SIGHTSEEING

J.F.K. National Historic Site
➕ B5 ✉ 83 Beals Street
☎ 617/566–7937
🕐 May–Oct: Wed–Sun
10–4.30 🚇 Coolidge Corner
(green line C)

Frederick Law Olmsted National Historic Site
Landscaped gardens.
Weekend walking tours in autumn.
➕ C8 ✉ 99 Warren Street
☎ 617/566–1689 🕐 Fri–Sun
10–4.30 🚇 Brookline Hills
(green line D) then 1.2km
(0.75-mile) walk.

Museum of Transportation
In Larz Anderson Park
➕ A10 ✉ 15 Newton Street,
Brookline ☎ 617/522–6547
🕐 Tue–Sun, Mon hols, and in vacation weeks 10–5
🚇 Cleveland Circle (green line C), then bus 51 (not Sun)

BOSTON TEA PARTY SHIP & MUSEUM

Board a replica Tea Party ship, stick a plastic feather in your hair, boo the Brits, and maybe get to throw a styrofoam tea chest into the sea—but be aware that there are other ways of learning about this significant event (► 42).
➕ H5 ✉ Congress Street Bridge ☎ 617/338–1773
🕐 Daily 9–5 (summer 9–6).
Closed 1 Dec–Feb 🍴 Nearby
🚇 South Station ♿ No wheelchair access to boat 💷 Expensive

CHILDREN'S MUSEUM (► 61)

DREAMS OF FREEDOM

A multi-media interactive telling of the story of Boston's immigrants.
➕ H4; cIV ✉ 1 Milk Street ☎ 617/338–6022 🕐 10–6 🚇 Park Street, State 💷 Moderate

GIBSON HOUSE MUSEUM

A virtually unchanged 1860 Back Bay family home, with a super collection of Victoriana.
➕ G5 ✉ 137 Beacon Street ☎ 617/267–6338
🕐 Tours only, at 1, 2, 3PM, Wed–Sun. Also by appointment
🚇 Arlington ♿ No wheelchair access 💷 Moderate

INSTITUTE OF CONTEMPORARY ART (ICA)

An exhibition, film, and performance space in a 19th-century police and fire station.
Whatever's on is likely to be innovative.
➕ F5 ✉ 955 Boylston Street (at Hereford Street); plans to move to Waterfront in 2005 ☎ 617/266–5152
🕐 Wed–Sun noon–5 (Thu until 9) 🚇 Hynes Convention Center/ICA 💷 Moderate; free Thu 5–9

J.F.K.'s birthplace, Brookline

MIT MUSEUMS

The main MIT exhibition space has a unique collection of holograms. It is also home to the Hall of Hacks, featuring MIT student pranks (on display is the police car found on top of the MIT Dome in May 1994). Flashes of Inspiration explores the work of MIT legend Harold "Doc" Edgerton, who made the invisible visible. See his sequential photos of a balloon bursting.

The Hart Nautical Collections, in the main campus, cover the technical side of naval architecture with exquisite ship models. The List Visual Art Center exhibits cutting-edge work.

🏛 E4 ✉ 265 Massachusetts Avenue, Cambridge
☎ 617/253–4444 🕐 Tue–Fri 10–5; Sat, Sun noon–5
Ⓜ Central, then walk ◑ Inexpensive

Hart Nautical Gallery 🏛 E4 ✉ 55 Massachusetts Avenue
☎ 617/253–5942 🕐 Daily 9–8 Ⓜ Kendall ◑ Free

List Visual Art Center 🏛 E4 ✉ 20 Ames Street ☎ 617/253–4400 🕐 Tue–Sun noon–6 (Fri until 8) Ⓜ Kendall ◑ Free

MUSEUM OF AFRO-AMERICAN HISTORY/BLACK HERITAGE TRAIL

A museum dedicated to the history of African Americans in Boston is housed in the African Meeting House, built in 1806 and the oldest surviving African-American church building in the US. Once a centre for social and political activity, it is now a focal point on the Black Heritage Trail, a 2.5km (1.6-mile) guided or self-guided walking tour of pre-Civil War Beacon Hill sites, including the Abiel Smith School and the Robert Gould Shaw Monument (▶ 57).

🏛 bIII; G4 ✉ 46 Joy Street ☎ 617/725–0022 🕐 Memorial Day–Labor Day: daily 10–4. Rest of year: Mon–Fri 10–4
Ⓜ Charles, Park Street, Bowdoin ◑ Free

NICHOLS HOUSE MUSEUM

One of Boston's earliest Federal-style houses, this elegant four-floor Beacon Hill house was built by Charles Bulfinch (▶ 11, 37) in 1804 and is furnished with Nichols family art and antiques.

🏛 bIII–IV; G4 ✉ 55 Mount Vernon Street ☎ 617/227–6993
🕐 May–Oct: Tue–Sat noon–4. Nov, Dec, Feb–Apr: Thu–Sat noon–4. By tour only; last tour 4 Ⓜ Park Street ◑ Moderate

PHOTOGRAPHIC RESOURCE CENTER

Good exhibition for photography enthusiasts—in the basement of a Boston University building.

🏛 D5 ✉ 602 Commonwealth Avenue ☎ 617/353–0700
🕐 Tue–Sun noon–5 (Thu until 8) Ⓜ Boston University East
◑ Inexpensive (free on Thu PM)

TRACING YOUR ANCESTORS

New England Historic Genealogical Society
Did your ancestors come over on the *Mayflower*? Get help with your research here.

🏛 F5 ✉ 99 Newbury Street
☎ 617/536–5740 🕐 Tue–Sat 9–5 (Thu till 9) Ⓜ Copley

Harold Edgerton's Milkdrop Coronet in his Flashes of Inspiration exhibit at MIT Museum

Skyscrapers and 20th-Century Buildings

Downtown view, Kilby Street, near State Street

AMES AND SEARS BUILDINGS

The 14-floor 1889 Ames Building dominated the skyline until the Custom House Tower was built.
✚ dIII; H4 ✉ 1 Court Street 🚇 State

CUSTOM HOUSE TOWER

The 30-floor clock tower (1915) is a Boston landmark and was for a long time the city's tallest building. At street level you see how silly it looks stuck on the roof of the original Custom House, built in 1847 in Greek Revival style, at what was then the water's edge. It is now a hotel, but the public can go up to the observatory for great views.
✚ dIII; H4 ✉ 3 McKinley Square 🕐 Observatory daily at 10 and 4, except Sat AM 🚇 State, Aquarium 🎟 Donation to charity

MIT BUILDINGS

MIT has some impressive modern architecture. You are free to wander around the campus. Seek out Eero Saarinen's serene round chapel (1955), near the Student Center on Massachusetts Avenue. Overlooking the river nearby, the student dorm Baker House (1947) is by Finnish architect Alvar Aalto, while on and near Ames Street the low Wiesner and the tall Green buildings are the work of I. M. Pei (1964, 1985).
✚ E4 ✉ Massachusetts Avenue, Memorial Drive, Ames Street 🚇 Kendall

ART DECO SKYSCRAPERS

There are four landmark Art deco buildings in and around Post Office Square. On the corner of Water and Congress, note the elaborate facade of the John W. McCormack Post Office and Court House (1931). In Federal Street (at Franklin), the old State Street Bank, 70–75, has an external metalwork frieze and splendid metalwork in the lobby at 75–101. At 160 Federal the United Shoe Machinery Building (1929) has exciting metalwork in and out. Also, look for No. 60 Battery-march Street, now Wyndham Boston Hotel (1928).
✚ dIV; H5 ☎ State, Downtown Crossing, Aquarium

VERIZON BUILDING

This 1940s art deco structure (formerly the Bell Atlantic/New England Telephone building) dominates Post Office Square. In the lobby, a 1950s mural (by Dean Cornwell) and a re-creation of Alexander Graham Bell's workshop celebrate the invention (in Boston) of the telephone.
✚ dIV; H5 ✉ 185 Franklin ☎ State, Downtown Crossing 🎟 Free

Statues, Monuments & Sculptures

SAM ADAMS
Anne Whitney's (1880) portrayal of the defiant revolutionary leader, in front of Faneuil Hall.
➕ dIII; H4 ✉ Congress Street 🚇 State

IRISH FAMINE MEMORIAL
These 1998 bronzes commemorate those forced by the 1840s Potato Famine to leave their native Ireland.
➕ cIV; H4 ✉ Washington/School streets

JAMES CURLEY
A colourful Boston Irish mayor, Curley (1874–1958) comes seated and standing (Lloyd Lillie, 1980).
➕ dIII; H4 ✉ North/Union Street 🚇 State

MAKE WAY FOR DUCKLINGS (► 61)

MIT SCULPTURES
On the campus are two Henry Moore reclining figure pieces (1963, 1976), Alexander Calder's black steel *The Big Sail* (1965), and Michael Heizer's pink granite *Guennette* (1977).
➕ E4 ✉ Memorial Drive 🕐 Daily 🚇 Kendall
🆓 Free

NEW ENGLAND HOLOCAUST MEMORIAL
Six tall glass towers, the work of Stanley Saitowitz (1995), recall Nazi death camps. Etched numerals represent the Holocaust's 6 million victims. The memorial is especially poignant after dark, when it is floodlit.
➕ dIII; H4 ✉ Union Street 🚇 State

PAUL REVERE
A bronze equestrian statue (1940) of the legendary figure (► 17) by Cyrus Dallin.
➕ dII; H4 ✉ Paul Revere Mall, North End 🚇 State, Aquarium, North Station

ROBERT GOULD SHAW MONUMENT
A sensitive bronze battle frieze by Augustus Saint-Gaudens (1897). Shaw, depicted in the film *Glory*, led the Union's first black regiment off to battle in the Civil War. Here, for the first time, blacks were portrayed by a white artist as individuals.
➕ bIV; G4 ✉ Beacon Street, facing State House 🚇 Park

ART ON THE T

MBTA (Massachusetts Bay Transportation Authority) has an enlightened policy of installing works of art in its subway stations. Keep an eye out, for example, for the layered hands sculpture and the ceramic mural in Park Street Station, the granite benches placed randomly on the platforms at Downtown Crossing, or the multicoloured "Omphaios" sculpture outside Harvard Square station.

Statue of Paul Revere

Places of Worship & Burial Grounds

MOUNT AUBURN CEMETERY, CAMBRIDGE

A little out of the way, but a beautiful place. It was built in 1831 as the country's first rural garden cemetery and is still very popular with bird and plant lovers. If it's a nice day you could walk from Longfellow House (➤ 26). Longfellow now rests here, as does artist Winslow Homer.
✚ B2 ✉ Mount Auburn Street, Cambridge
☎ 617/547–7105 ⏱ Daily
🚇 Harvard, then walk or Watertown bus

AFRICAN MEETING HOUSE (➤ 55)

ARLINGTON STREET CHURCH

If the church is closed, ask the staff in the office (at the back) if it can be opened up. It has the largest collection of Tiffany windows in any one church.
✚ G5 ✉ Boylston Street at Arlington Street. Office: 351 Boylston Street ⏱ Office: Mon–Thu 9–4 🚇 Arlington

COPP'S HILL BURYING GROUND

Rows of carved skulls have good all-round views from this old Native American lookout point in the North End. Puritans Increase and Cotton Mather are buried here.
✚ dI; H3 ✉ Hull Street ⏱ Daily 🚇 North Station

KING'S CHAPEL AND BURYING GROUND

This was built as an Anglican church in 1687 on the orders of King James II, to the indignation of the Puritan colonists. In the town's earliest (1630) burial ground lie two *Mayflower* passengers and John Winthrop, first governor of Massachusetts.
✚ cIV; H4 ✉ Tremont/School streets 🚇 Park

Park Street Church

OLD GRANARY BURYING GROUND

If you see only one burial ground, make it this one. Dating back to 1660, it's the leafy resting place of many of Boston's big names—Samuel Adams, Paul Revere, James Otis, John Hancock, Peter Faneuil. A board explains the wonderful headstone carvings.
✚ cIV; H4 ✉ 88 Tremont Street ⏱ Daily 🚇 Park

PARK STREET CHURCH

Notable as much for its tall white steeple as for William Lloyd Garrison's first anti-slavery speech made here in 1829. "America the Beautiful" was first sung here in 1831.
✚ cIV; H4 ✉ 1 Park Street ⏱ Jul–Aug: daily 🚇 Park

Parks & Retreats

ARNOLD ARBORETUM
Stunning in all seasons, this is a rolling hilly park that's well worth the trip to the suburbs. Part of Olmsted's Emerald Necklace (► panel).
➕ B10 ✉ 125 Arborway, Jamaica Plain ☎ 617/524–1718 Ⓜ Orange line to Forest Hills 🎫 Free

BACK BAY FENS
The Back Bay Fens was the first of Olmsted's string of parks (► panel). Tall rushes line the Muddy River banks behind the Museum of Fine Arts; stroll through the willows or sit in the Rose Garden.
➕ E6 ✉ The Fenway/Park Drive Ⓜ Museum, Hynes

CHARLES RIVER: ESPLANADE AND BOAT TOURS
A favourite for roller blading, jogging, sunbathing, and more (► 60 biking, boating). Free summer concerts in Hatch Shell (► 80). Also open-air film screenings. Charles River Boat Tours leave from CambridgeSide near the Science Museum.
Esplanade ➕ F5 ✉ Storrow Memorial Drive Ⓜ Charles/MGH
Riverboat Tours ➕ G3 ✉ 100 CambridgeSide ☎ 617/621–3001 🕐 Memorial Day–Labor Day: daily. Apr, May, Oct: Sat, Sun Ⓜ Lechmere

CHRISTOPHER COLUMBUS PARK
This is a small waterfront park near Faneuil Hall Marketplace and North End. Buy a sandwich, sit under the trellis or on the grass, and watch the boats.
➕ eIII; H4 ✉ Atlantic Avenue Ⓜ Aquarium

POST OFFICE SQUARE (► 56)
A charming downtown oasis, with a small café.
➕ dIV; H5 ✉ Between Milk and Franklin streets Ⓜ State

THE EMERALD NECKLACE

So called because it resembles a string of beads, Boston's interconnecting chain of parks was designed in 1895, when such things were a novel idea, by America's first landscape architect, Frederick Law Olmsted. The gardens of Commonwealth Avenue link Boston Common and the Public Garden with the Back Bay Fens. From here it is possible to walk along the reed-fringed Riverway to Olmsted Park and on to Jamaica Pond, a popular spot for fishing and boating. Arnold Arboretum (► left) is 0.8km (0.5 miles) away and then there's Franklin Park, with a zoo (► 61). In the autumn the Frederick Law Olmsted National Historic Site (► 54) leads weekend walks through the Emerald Necklace.

Autumn colours on the Charles River Esplanade

Sport & Outdoor Activities

Sailing on the Charles River

THE MAJOR VENUES

Fenway Park for Red Sox
⊞ E6 ✉ 24 Yawkey Way
☎ Tickets: 617/267–1700 or
Ticketmaster 617/931–2000.
Tours: 617/236–6666;
www.redsox.com
🚇 Kenmore Square

FleetCenter for Celtics and Bruins
⊞ cl; H3 ✉ 150 Causeway
Street ☎ Ticketmaster:
617/931–2000;
www.fleetcenter.com
🚇 North Station

Foxboro Stadium for Patriots and NE Revolution
⊞ Off B10 ✉ Rte 1
Foxborough ☎ Ticketmaster:
617/931–2000;
www.foxboro.com

Tickets can also be bought at
BosTix stalls in Faneuil Hall
Marketplace and Copley
Square, or in person at venue
box offices.

AMERICAN FOOTBALL/ MEN'S SOCCER
Foxboro (an hour's drive south or the train from South Station) is home to the New England Patriots from August to September, and the men's pro soccer team, New England Revolution, from April to July.

BASEBALL/FENWAY PARK
The Boston Red Sox play from April to October. Aged, cramped, and idiosyncratic, Fenway is famous for its Green Monster, the high left-field wall—there are plans to rebuild the stadium, so if you want to see it, go to a match or take a tour soon.

BASKETBALL/FLEETCENTER
The Boston Celtics play here from October to May.

BIKING, IN-LINE SKATING, AND JOGGING
The Esplanade is always popular. On spring and summer Sundays part of Memorial Drive, on the Cambridge side of the river, is closed to vehicles, so you can walk, cycle, or skate along one bank, cross on any bridge and return on the other. For bicycle and in-line skate rental ► 76 (panel).

BOATING
Canoes, kayaks, and sailing dinghies can be rented at the Charles River Esplanade.

THE BOSTON MARATHON
Started in 1897, the first marathon in the US, and the world's oldest annual event, this 42km (26.2-mile) run (Hopkinton to Copley Square) takes place on the third Monday in April (Patriots' Day).

HEAD OF THE CHARLES REGATTA
Thousands come, often with picnics, for this major international rowing event in October.

ICE HOCKEY
The NHL's illustrious Boston Bruins play at FleetCenter (October to April). The Beanpot inter-collegiate tournament is held in early February.

ICE SKATING
In winter, on Frog Pond on Boston Common.
☎ 617/635–2120 ❓ Rent skates from the booth

Things for Children to See & Do

Children love the street performers in Faneuil Hall Marketplace, and there are souvenir shops and sweet stands too. Harvard Square also has plenty of entertainment. Whale-watching trips, Duck Tours, and Swan Boats (► 48, 20, 38) are popular, as are the Mapparium (► 31) and Prudential Skywalk (► 32). Sports enthusiasts will want to tour Fenway Park (► 60) or the FleetCenter's Sports Museum (☎ 617/624–1234). The museums and galleries often have activities laid on for children; at the Museum of Fine Arts (► 30), you can leave your children happily occupied in the children's room while you make your visit in peace (☎ 617/369–3300 ☻ Mon–Fri 3.30–4.45).

BOSTON TEA PARTY SHIP & MUSEUM (► 54)

CHILDREN'S MUSEUM
This museum is heaven on earth for the under-10s. Try the balance climb, play at shops with life-size products, squirt water jets at model boats, stretch a gigantic bubble, or just have fun in the play space. And when you're all exhausted, retreat to the peace and quiet of the Japanese house.
✚ J5 ✉ 300 Congress Street, Museum Wharf ☎ 617/426–8855 ☻ Daily 10–5 (Fri until 9) 🍴 McDonald's adjoins 🚇 South Station 💰 Moderate (Fri 5–9 $1)

FRANKLIN PARK ZOO
Wander through an African Tropical Forest, stroke small animals at the Children's Zoo, visit the lions, then picnic in the hills and meadows.
✚ E10 ✉ 1 Franklin Park Road ☎ 617/442–2002 ☻ Daily 🍴 Café or picnic 🚇 Forest Hills, then bus 16 💰 Moderate; under 4s free

MIT MUSEUMS (► 55)

PLIMOTH PLANTATION (► 20)

PUPPET SHOWPLACE THEATER (► 83)

PLAYGROUNDS

There are good playgrounds where young children can let off steam: on Boston Common, on the Charles River Esplanade, in the Waterfront Columbus Park (not far from the Aquarium), in Clarendon Street in the South End, and on Cambridge Common.

"MAKE WAY FOR DUCKLINGS"

Look for the mother duck and ducklings in the Public Garden, a bronze sculpture based on Robert McCloskey's famous book. The same artist, Nancy Schon, created the hare and tortoise, who mark the spot where the Boston Marathon ends in Copley Square.

Make way for ducklings!

Freebies & Cheapies

A Boston Pops concert in the Hatch Shell

PLACES OF INTEREST WITH FREE ENTRY

- African Meeting House (➤ 55)
- Boston Athenaeum (➤ 41)
- Boston Public Library (➤ 33)
- Bunker Hill Monument (➤ 45)
- Charlestown Navy Yard ships and museum (➤ 45)
- First Church of Christ, Scientist, Mary Baker Eddy Library, and Mapparium (➤ 31)
- Churches and burial grounds (➤ 58)
- Commonwealth Museum, history and people of Massachusetts ✉ 220 Morrissey Boulevard, Columbia Point ☎ 617/727-9268 ⊙ Mon–Fri 9–5; Sat 9–3, except hols
- Faneuil Hall (➤ 44)
- Ether Dome, Bulfinch Pavilion, Massachusetts General Hospital (➤ 53) ✉ Blossom Street ☎ 617/726-2000 ⊙ 9–8 except during a conference
- Harvard University museums at certain times (➤ 28)
- ICA Thu 5–9 (➤ 54)
- Massachusetts State House (➤ 40)
- MIT's List Visual Art Center and Hart Nautical Galleries (➤ 55)
- Photographic Resource Center Thu noon–8 (➤ 55)
- Verizon (Bell Atlantic) Building mural and Alexander Bell Museum (➤ 56)

SPECIAL ADMISSION CHARGES

Several places offer reduced-price entry at certain times. The Museum of Fine Arts is pay-as-you-wish Wednesday 4–9.45. Admission to the Children's Museum is $1 Friday 5–9. A donation to charity gets you up to the Custom House Tower Observatory.

FESTIVALS

Check in the *Boston Globe* or *Phoenix* for free events, from summer festivals in the Italian North End and 4th of July fireworks on the Esplanade to Christmas tree lighting ceremonies at the Prudential Center and First Night celebrations on New Year's Eve.

MUSICAL ENTERTAINMENT

The ever-popular Boston Pops orchestra holds free concerts in July in the Hatch Shell on the Esplanade (➤ 80). Concerts at the New England Conservatory are free (➤ 80). The Boston Symphony Orchestra has inexpensive open rehearsals. See the *Boston Globe* or *Phoenix*. Trinity Church (➤ 81) holds free organ recitals Fridays 12.15. The Federal Reserve Bank of Boston hosts free concerts most Thursdays, September to December and March to June, at 12.30.
Federal Reserve Bank of Boston ➕ H5 ✉ 600 Atlantic Avenue (opposite South Station) ☎ 617/913–3453

PARKS AND OPEN SPACES

It doesn't cost anything to enjoy the places described under Parks and Retreats (➤ 59). Boston Common, the Public Garden, and the Esplanade are popular year-round. Public spaces all over the city are notably rich in sculptures, murals, and other art installations.

BOSTON
where to

The Best of Boston

PRICES

Approximate prices for a two-course meal for one with a drink:

$ up to $20
$$ up to $40
$$$ more than $40

BOSTON CLASSICS

Timeless institutions include:
Durgin Park
One of the oldest dining rooms in the US. The roast beef melts in the mouth and there's hard-to-find traditional fare like Indian pudding. Crowded; very informal—but the waiters make a thing of being rude.
✉ Faneuil Hall Marketplace
☎ 617/227–2038;
www.durgin-park.com
Locke-Ober
Originally a gentlemen's club, and still feels like one. Now run by Lydia Shire.
Old-fashioned menu updated with contemporary flourishes.
✉ 3 Winter Place
☎ 617/542–1340
◷ Mon–Fri lunch, dinner; Sat dinner
Union Oyster House
Said to be the oldest restaurant in the US; on the Freedom Trail. Boston scrod is a local favourite.
✉ 41 Union Street, Faneuil Hall
☎ 617/227–2750;
www.unionoysterhouse.com
◷ From 11

AMBROSIA ON HUNTINGTON ($$$)

The unconventional menu at this hip, postmodern spot blends French, Italian, and Asian in bold new dishes: Try the pig chop with Japanese forbidden rice and honey-galangal sauce.
➕ F6 ✉ 116 Huntington Avenue, Back Bay ☎ 617/247–2400; www.ambrosiaon huntington.com ◷ Lunch Mon–Fri; dinner daily
Ⓜ Prudential

AUJOURD'HUI ($$$)

Overlooking the Public Garden and known as much for the service as the food, this is one of Boston's best formal restaurants. The chef's complex presentations and unusual combinations are pricey, but overall, it's close to perfect.
➕ G5 ✉ Four Seasons Hotel, 200 Boylston Street, Back Bay ☎ 617/451–1392;
www.fourseasons.com/boston/dining ◷ Lunch Mon–Fri; dinner daily; brunch Sun Ⓜ Arlington

BLU ($$$)

Creative contemporary fare in an airy room in a health club near the Theater District. Seafood, including an elaborate raw bar, stands out.
➕ G5 ✉ Sports Club/LA, 4 Avery Street ☎ 617/375–8550 ◷ Mon–Fri lunch; Mon–Sat dinner; Sun brunch Ⓜ Boylston

CHEZ HENRI ($$$)

Trendy French/Cuban cuisine in a storefront bistro between Harvard and Porter Squares. Eclectic but wonderful.
➕ C2 ✉ 1 Shepard Street at Massachusetts Avenue ☎ 617/354–8980 ◷ Daily dinner
Ⓜ Harvard then bus 77 or walk

CLIO ($$$)

Excellent contemporary fare that's creative without being weird. A fine choice for business entertaining. The leopard-print rug adds just the right level of "chic" to an otherwise sedate dining room. Good seafood preparations include chilled lobster and scallops with hot-and-sour bell-pepper broth.
➕ E5 ✉ Eliot Hotel, 370a Commonwealth Avenue, Back Bay ☎ 617/536–7200;
www.eliothotel.com ◷ Daily dinner Ⓜ Hynes/ICA

THE ELEPHANT WALK ($$)

Intriguing Cambodian and French food. Popular with students and young trendies.
➕ D6 ✉ 900 Beacon Street ☎ 617/247–1500; www.elephantwalk.com ◷ Mon–Fri lunch; daily dinner Ⓜ St. Mary's Street (green line C);
➕ Off map at 1C ✉ 2067 Massachusetts Avenue, Cambridge ☎ 617/492–6900 ◷ Daily dinner Ⓜ Porter, then walk

HAMERSLEY'S BISTRO ($$$)

Excellent American-French cooking in an informal setting. Refreshingly simple preparations such as cassoulet or roast chicken with garlic and lemon.
➕ G6 ✉ 553 Tremont Street (at Clarendon), South End ☎ 617/423–2700;
www.hamersleybistro.com ◷ Dinner Ⓜ Back Bay

JULIEN ($$$)

Very French, very formal, very pricey, but superb. Not for those easily intimidated by the rituals of fine dining or those with an aversion to butter.
➕ dIV; H5 ✉ Le Meridien Hotel, 250 Franklin Street, Financial District ☎ 617/451–1900; www.lemeridienboston.com ⏱ Mon–Sat dinner Ⓜ State, Downtown Crossing

L'ESPALIER ($$$)

Superb contemporary fare in the formal and romantic setting of a 19th-century Back Bay house. Prix fixe.
➕ F5 ✉ 30 Gloucester Street, Back Bay ☎ 617/262–3023; www.lespalier.com ⏱ Mon–Sat dinner Ⓜ Hynes/ICA

MAISON ROBERT ($$$)

As French as the name, the agreeable food at this Boston mainstay is old-fashioned, though not without contemporary flourishes; the wine list is impressive, if expensive.
➕ cIV; H4 ✉ 45 School Street, Downtown ☎ 617/227–3370; www.maisonrobert.com ⏱ Mon–Fri lunch, dinner; Sat dinner Ⓜ State, Park Street

MANTRA ($$$)

Exotic French-Indian fusion fare in a high-style former bank. Expert service. Lively bar scene, complete with hookah den.
➕ cIV; H5 ✉ 52 Temple Place, Downtown ☎ 617/542–8111 ⏱ Mon–Sat lunch, dinner Ⓜ Park, Downtown Crossing

MISTRAL ($$$)

One of Boston's hippest dining rooms, a see-and-be-seen kind of place. Dramatic (but noisy) room, contemporary cuisine (grilled portobello mushroom "carpaccio" with roasted peppers).
➕ G5 ✉ 223 Columbus Avenue ☎ 617/867–9300; www.mistralbistro.com ⏱ Sun–Thu 5.30–10.30; Fri–Sat 5.30–11.30 Ⓜ Arlington, Back Bay

NO. 9 PARK ($$$)

New American fare in a dignified if simple dining room. Chef Barbara Lynch has a way with duck; her signature crispy duck is deliciously crisp outside, meltingly tender within. Less expensive bar menu.
➕ bIV; G4 ✉ 9 Park Street, downtown ☎ 617/742–9991 ⏱ Mon–Fri lunch; Mon–Sat dinner Ⓜ Park

OLIVES ($$$)

Inventive Mediterranean-influenced cooking in this restaurant owned by chef Todd English; bold flavours, huge portions. Reservations for 6 or more; otherwise expect a wait.
➕ H3 ✉ 10 City Square, Charlestown ☎ 617/242–1999 ⏱ Mon–Sat dinner Ⓜ North Station, then walk; Haymarket, then bus 92 or 93

RADIUS ($$$)

Culinary hotspot set in a 1920s one-time downtown bank. Chef Michael Schlow serves modern French cuisine: roasted halibut with cauliflower purée and lentils, venison in green peppercorn sauce.
➕ dV; H5 ✉ 8 High Street, Financial District ☎ 617/426–1234; www.radiusrestaurant.com ⏱ Mon–Fri lunch; Mon–Sat dinner Ⓜ South Station

HOT DISTRICTS

Boston's hottest restaurant district is the South End. And keep an eye on Somerville, north of Cambridge. In the South End:

Aquitaine
Popular upscale French bistro and wine bar.
✉ 569 Tremont Street ☎ 617/424–8577; www.aquitaineboston.com

Truc
Tiny spot; creative French cuisine.
✉ 560 Tremont Street ☎ 617/338–8070

Tremont 647
Adventurous new American/fusion food; casually hip room. "Pajama Brunch" on Sunday.
✉ 647 Tremont Street ☎ 617/266–4600; www.tremont647.com

In Somerville:

The Burren
Davis Square Irish pub. Good fish and chips. Music on several nights.
✉ 247 Elm Street ☎ 617/776–6896; www.burren.com

eat
Updated American classics in a small, unadorned Union Square room.
✉ 253 Washington Street ☎ 617/776–2889

EVOO
Despite the unusual name (it stands for Extra Virgin Olive Oil), the eclectic fare at this stylish little bistro is first-rate.
✉ 118 Beacon Street ☎ 617/661–3866

Seafood

MORE SEAFOOD OPTIONS

Nowadays some of Boston's finest fish is served outside of the traditional seafood restaurants listed on this page. Most of the city's best eating spots do an excellent job with seafood preparations, and these dishes are taking an increasingly large share of their menus.

Other good choices for fresh seafood are any of the Chinatown restaurants with live-from-the-tanks fish.

FOR LANDLUBBERS ONLY: HOW TO EAT A LOBSTER

1 Put the bib on.
2 Break the claws off.
3 Use the nutcracker to open them.
4 Bend the back until the tailpiece splits off.
5 Break the flippers off the tail.
6 Push the meat out of the tail with the thin fork.
7 Pull the back out of the body. You may not want to eat the liver.
8 Crack open the rest of the body sideways (the best meat is here).
9 Suck the meat out of the little claw.

ANTHONY'S PIER 4 ($$)

Big, busy restaurant on the Fish Pier, with views. Traditional (if unexciting) seafood. Jackets advisable.
⊞ J5 ⊠ 140 Northern Avenue, Waterfront ☎ 617/423–6363; www.pier4.com
⏱ Mon–Fri from 11.30; Sat, Sun from noon Ⓜ South Station

BARKING CRAB ($)

A rough-and-ready clam shack where you can eat indoors or alfresco, with downtown views across the water. Expect crowds, a wait, noise, and fun.
⊞ J5 ⊠ 88 Sleeper Street, off Northern Avenue, Waterfront ☎ 617/426–2722 ⏱ From 11.30 Ⓜ South Station

EAST COAST GRILL & RAW BAR ($$–$$$)

Wildly popular seafood and barbecue joint. Fresh seafood often served with intriguing spice rubs and fruit salsas. Reservations Sunday to Thursday for parties of five or more.
⊞ E3 ⊠ 1271 Cambridge Street, Inman Square ☎ 617/491–6568; www.eastcoastgrill. net ⏱ Daily dinner; Sun brunch Ⓜ Central, then long walk or bus 83 to Inman Square; Harvard then bus 69 on Cambridge Street

JASPER WHITE'S SUMMER SHACK ($$–$$$)

You eat at picnic tables inside this cavernous fish house. It is informal and loud, but chef Jasper White knows his lobster.
⊞ Off map at A1 ⊠ 149 Alewife Brook Parkway, Fresh Pond ☎ 617/520–9500; www.summershackrestaurant.com ⏱ Mon–Fri lunch; daily dinner Ⓜ Alewife

JIMMY'S HARBORSIDE ($$)

Fine old institution—good fish and solid steak dishes, a first-class wine list, and excellent waterfront views.
⊞ J5 ⊠ 242 Northern Avenue, Waterfront ☎ 617/423–1000; jimmysharborside. com ⏱ From noon; Sun dinner Ⓜ South Station

KINGFISH HALL ($$–$$$)

Flashy Faneuil Hall fish joint, owned by Todd English. Creative, if pricey, fish dishes in an eclectic modern (and noisy) room.
⊞ dlll; H4 ⊠ 188 S. Market Street ☎ 617/523–8862; www.toddenglish.com ⏱ Mon–Sat lunch; dinner daily; Sun brunch Ⓜ State, Government Center

LEGAL SEA FOODS ($$)

Popular seafood chain serving straightforward, reliably good fish. Makes a decent clam chowder.
⊠ 255 State Street; 26 Park Square; Prudential Center; Copley Place; 5 Cambridge Center, Kendall Square ☎ 617/227–3115; 617/426–4444; 617/266–6800; 617/266–7775; 617/864–3400; www.legalseafoods.com ⏱ Hours vary Ⓜ Aquarium; Arlington; Prudential; Copley; Kendall

TURNER FISHERIES ($$)

The acclaimed seafood restaurant in the Westin Hotel prides itself on its clam chowder, so this has to be your benchmark.
⊞ F5 ⊠ The Westin Hotel, Copley Place, 10 Huntington Avenue ☎ 617/424–7425 ⏱ Daily dinner Ⓜ Copley

Italian & Mediterranean

ARTÙ ($)
Country-style Italian cooking. Friendly and informal. Try chicken layered with eggplant and mozzarella. Also at 89 Charles Street.
✚ dll; H4 ✉ 6 Prince Street, North End ☎ 617/742–4336 🕐 From 11 🚇 Haymarket

CAFFÉ UMBRA ($$–$$$)
Casual-chic South End trattoria with a modern French-Italian menu. Striking view of the cathedral of the Holy Cross, across the street.
✚ G6 ✉ 1395 Washington Street ☎ 617/867– 0707 🕐 Dinner Tue–Sat 🚇 Back Bay

CANTINA ITALIANA ($)
A relaxed eatery serving excellent regional food.
✚ dll; H4 ✉ 346 Hanover Street, North End ☎ 617/723–4577 🕐 Mon–Sat from 4; Sun from noon 🚇 Haymarket

CENTRO ($$)
Contemporary fare that travels the Italian regions in a 30-seat Central Square trattoria. Excellent value. Enter through the Good Life bar next door.
✚ D3 ✉ 720 Massachusetts Avenue, Central Square ☎ 617/868–2405; www.centrocambridge.com 🕐 Daily dinner 🚇 Central

MAMMA MARIA ($$$)
Highly regarded elegant North End Italian, offering imaginative cooking and gracious service. Try the *osso buco* (traditional shin of veal stew).
✚ dll; H4 ✉ 3 North Square, North End ☎ 617/523–0077; www.mammamaria.com 🕐 Daily dinner 🚇 Haymarket

MARCUCCIO'S ($$$)
Contemporary Italian fare in a funky storefront. Chef Roberto Dias creates light but lusty dishes, such as fusilli with smoked pancetta, black olives, and sautéed greens, or striped bass with parsley purée.
✚ dll; H4 ✉ 125 Salem Street, North End ☎ 617/723–1807; www.marcuccios.com 🕐 Daily dinner 🚇 Haymarket

PREZZA ($$$)
Modern Italian fare in a hip space. Try the homemade pastas such as pea tortelli with Virginia ham. Save room for the chocolate hazelnut cake. Happening bar scene too.
✚ d–ell; H4 ✉ 24 Fleet Street, North End ☎ 617/227–1577; www.prezza.com 🕐 Mon–Sat dinner 🚇 Haymarket

RISTORANTE TOSCANO ($$$)
One of the best, this elegant eatery has a genuine Italian ambience and an excellent wine list.
✚ aIV; G4 ✉ 47 Charles Street, Beacon Hill ☎ 617/723–4090; www.ristorantetoscanoboston.com 🕐 Mon–Sat lunch; dinner daily 🚇 Charles/MGH

TAPEO ($$)
Surreal Spanish restaurant and tapas bar. Very popular. Be prepared to wait.
✚ F5 ✉ 266 Newbury Street, Back Bay ☎ 617/267–4799; www.tapeorestaurant.com 🕐 Sat, Sun lunch; daily dinner 🚇 Hynes/ICA

DINING WITH A VIEW

Bay Tower Room
Look down on the city and harbour from 33 floors up. New American cuisine.
✉ 60 State Street, Faneuil Hall ☎ 617/723–1666; www.baytower.com

Joe's American Bar & Grill
Regional American dishes, right on the water's edge.
✉ 100 Atlantic Avenue, Waterfront ☎ 617/367–8700; www.joesamerican.com

Seasons
Luxury rooftop with views over Faneuil Hall; new American cuisine.
✉ Millennium Bostonian Hotel, Faneuil Hall Marketplace ☎ 617/523–4149; www.millennium-hotels.com

Top of the Hub
The highest dining room in Boston, on the 52nd floor of the Prudential Tower. Also light (and less expensive) meals served in the lounge till late.
✉ Prudential Center, Boylston Street ☎ 617/536–1775

Also worth trying: Aujourd'hui (► 64); Anthony's Pier 4, Barking Crab (► 66); Skyline, Museum of Science (► 70)

67

American & Mexican

NEW ENGLAND DISHES

Try these: lobster, clam chowder, scrod, *quahog* (a large clam, pronounced "ko hog"), Boston baked beans (cooked long and slow in an earthenware pot), Boston cream pie (chocolate-covered and custard-filled), Indian pudding (cornmeal, milk, and molasses, cooked long and slow).

BEER HERE!

Brewpubs are popular spots, especially before or after sports events. Try:
Boston Beer Works
✉ 61 Brookline Street, near Fenway Park; 112 Canal Street, near FleetCenter
☎ 617/536–2337; 617/896–2337

AMERICAN

GRILL 23 & BAR ($$$)

Steaks, prime rib of beef, lamb chops, swordfish, and more. Attentive service in a men's club-style room.
✚ G5 ✉ 161 Berkeley Street (at Stuart Street), Back Bay ☎ 617/542–2255; www.grill23.com ⏱ Dinner daily 🚇 Arlington

HENRIETTA'S TABLE ($$)

A country kitchen-style restaurant with creative New England food, and an all-American wine list.
✚ C3 ✉ Charles Hotel, 1 Bennett Street, Cambridge ☎ 617/661–5005; www.charleshotel.com ⏱ Daily breakfast, dinner; lunch Mon–Fri; brunch Sat, Sun 🚇 Harvard Square

HUNGRY I ($$$)

Tiny, intimate basement offering a small but inventive menu.
✚ aIV; G4 ✉ 71 Charles Street, Beacon Hill ☎ 617/227–3524 ⏱ Thu–Fri lunch; Tue–Sun dinner; Sun brunch 🚇 Charles Street

ICARUS ($$$)

Contemporary cooking (pepper-crusted venison with cranberries) in an elegant setting.
✚ G6 ✉ 3 Appleton Street, South End ☎ 617/426–1790; www.icarusrestaurant.com ⏱ Dinner daily 🚇 Back Bay

METROPOLIS CAFÉ ($$)

Honest contemporary food, (roast halibut with celery root purée; pork chop with crispy sage and mascarpone polenta).
✚ G6 ✉ 584 Tremont Street, South End ☎ 617/247–2931 ⏱ Dinner daily; Sat, Sun brunch 🚇 Back Bay

REDBONES ($)

A down-and-dirty rib joint, serving some of the area's best barbecued ribs. Excellent fried okra appetizer. Often crowded and boisterous. Interesting Microbrews on tap.
✚ Off map at C1 ✉ 55 Chester Street at Elm Street, Somerville ☎ 617/628–2200; www.redbonesbbq.com ⏱ Lunch, dinner 🚇 Davis

OAK ROOM ($$$)

Dark oak-panelled walls and well-spaced tables make for club-like privacy in the grande dame of Boston's hotels. It's a steak house—but the lobster bouillabaisse is also superb.
✚ F5 ✉ Fairmont Copley Plaza Hotel, Copley Square ☎ 617/267–5300; www.fairmont.com ⏱ Dinner daily 🚇 Copley

MEXICAN

BORDER CAFÉ ($)

This frenetic eatery serves competent Tex-Mex fare. Very popular with students.
✚ C2 ✉ 32 Church Street, Harvard Square ☎ 617/864–6100 ⏱ Lunch, dinner 🚇 Harvard Square

CASA ROMERO ($$)

Romantic eatery serving rich dishes such as chicken in a *mole poblano* (Poblano chilli) sauce. Eat alfresco in the courtyard.
✚ F5 ✉ 30 Gloucester Street, Back Bay ☎ 617/536–4341; www.casaromero.com ⏱ Dinner daily 🚇 Hynes/ICA

Asian & Middle Eastern

BOMBAY CLUB ($$)

Buffet lunch is excellent value in this comfortable Indian restaurant, but the view over Harvard Square is captivating anytime.

✚ C3 ✉ 57 J.F.K. Street, Harvard Square ☎ 617/661–8100; www.bombayclub.com 🕐 Mon–Fri lunch, dinner; Sat, Sun brunch, dinner 🚇 Harvard Square

GINZA ($$)

The "in" place for Japanese food.

✚ H5 ✉ 16 Hudson Street ☎ 617/338–2261 🕐 Lunch, dinner. Tue–Sat until 3.30AM; Sun, Mon until 2AM 🚇 Chinatown

GRAND CHAU CHOW ($)

Popular eatery serving Hong Kong-style food. Crowded dining room.

✚ H5 ✉ 45 Beach Street, Chinatown ☎ 617/292–5166 🕐 Lunch, dinner. Daily till 2AM 🚇 Chinatown

JAE'S ($$)

Always-busy Pan-Asian eatery. The house special dish is sushi. Also at 1281 Cambridge Street, Inman Square, Cambridge.

✚ F6 ✉ 520 Columbus Avenue, South End ☎ 617/421–9405 🕐 Mon–Sat lunch; dinner daily; brunch Sun 🚇 Prudential

NEW SHANGHAI ($)

More upscale than other Chinatown eateries, specializes in Shanghai-style cuisine. Unusual cold appetizers (sautéed eggplant with garlic sauce, hot and sour vegetables).

✚ H5 ✉ 21 Hudson Street ☎ 617/338–6688 🕐 Lunch, dinner 🚇 Chinatown

OLEANA ($$–$$$)

Ana Sortun experiments with intriguing Middle Eastern-Mediterranean flavours in her diminutive dining room. Sit on the pretty patio in summer.

✚ E3 ✉ 134 Hampshire Street, Cambridge ☎ 617/661–0505 🕐 Daily dinner 🚇 Harvard or Lechmere, then bus 69 on Cambridge Street to Prospect or Columbia streets

PHO PASTEUR ($)

Mini chain of Vietnamese eateries specializing in *pho* (beef noodle soup) and *bun* (vermicelli topped with meat or vegetables). The Theater District location has a more upscale menu.

✚ G5; G5; F5; C3 ✉ 682 Washington Street, Chinatown; 123 Stuart Street, Theater District; 119 Newbury Street, Back Bay; 36 J.F.K. Street, Harvard Square ☎ 617/482–7467; 617/742–2436; 617/262–8200; 617/864–4100; www.phopasteur boston.com 🚇 Chinatown; Boylston; Copley; Harvard

SULTAN'S KITCHEN ($)

This Turkish-Middle Eastern takeaway (with a few tables) is convenient for a quick lunch or early dinner; good vegetarian dishes, salads, and kebabs.

✚ dIV; H4 ✉ 72 Broad Street, Financial District ☎ 617/338–7819 🕐 Mon–Fri 11–8; Sat 11–3 🚇 Aquarium

THAI VILLAGE ($$)

Thai cuisine—lemon grass shrimp soup and mussel pancake—shines here.

✚ G6 ✉ 592 Tremont Street, South End ☎ 617/536–6548 🕐 Mon–Sat lunch; daily dinner 🚇 Back Bay

FOR VEGETARIANS

Boston is becoming increasingly vegetarian-friendly. More and more restaurants include at least one entrée, and many will make up a vegetarian plate on request.

In Chinatown try Buddha's Delight (✉ 3 Beach Street ☎ 617/451–2395). Downtown serves sophisticated vegetarian fare, as well as fish dishes. Milk Street Café (✉ 50 Milk Street, Financial District ☎ 617/542–3663) is a vegetarian-kosher luncheonette selling salads, soups, and vegetable sandwiches, plus meatless entrées.

In Cambridge, Casablanca (✉ 40 Brattle Street ☎ 617/876–0999) is a popular hangout for Harvard folk and young professionals, and serves good appetizers and Mediterranean fare. Veggie Planet (✚ Club Passim, 47 Palmer Street ☎ 617/661–1513; www.club passim.com) serves creative vegetarian pizzas in a Harvard Square folk-music club. Also try Border Café (► 68); Jae's, Sultan's Kitchen (► main entries, this page).

Brunch, Coffee, Tea & Late Eating

SUGGESTIONS FOR CHILDREN'S MEALS

Bertucci's
Local pizza-pasta chain.
✉ 21 Brattle Street, Harvard
Square, Cambridge
☎ 617/864–4748;
www.bertuccis.com;
✉ Faneuil Hall
☎ 617/227–7889

Figs
Gourmet pizzas and pastas.
✉ 42 Charles Street, Beacon
Hill ☎ 617/742–3447;
www.toddenglish.com;
✉ 67 Main Street,
Charlestown
☎ 617/242–2229

Hard Rock Café
A (loud) family favourite.
✉ 131 Clarendon Street, near
Hancock Tower
☎ 617/424–7625;
www.hardrock.com

Perennially popular is a *dim sum* lunch in Chinatown. Try
Chau Chow City (✉ 83 Essex
Street ☎ 617/338–8158) or
China Pearl (✉ 9 Tyler Street
☎ 617/426–4338). Skyline's
Sunday brunch at the Museum
of Science (☎ 617/723–2500)
overlooks the Charles River
and can be combined with a
movie in the IMAX cinema
(⊙ brunch at noon for a
screening at 2).

BRUNCH

Weekend brunch is
entrenched. Check out:
Aujourd'hui (➤ 64);
Sonsie (➤ 71); East Coast
Grill (➤ 66); Henrietta's
Table (➤ 68); Bombay
Club (➤ 69); Museum of
Science Skyline Brunch
(➤ this page, panel).

THE BLUE ROOM (SS–$$$)
This contemporary
American eatery in
Kendall Square serves
a bountiful Sunday brunch
buffet.
✚ E3 ✉ One Kendall Square
☎ 617/494–9034 ⊙ Dinner
daily; brunch Sun 🚇 Kendall

GARDNER MUSEUM CAFÉ ($)
Highly civilized weekend
brunch, preferably before
a (winter) afternoon
concert.
✚ D6 ✉ 280 The Fenway
☎ 617/566–1088;
www.gardnermuseum.org
⊙ Tue–Fri lunch 11.30–4; Sat,
Sun brunch 11–4 🚇 Museum

COFFEE

Branches of Au Bon Pain
("ABP") and Starbucks all
over town. Otherwise, try:

CAFFÈ PARADISO
Nice for an unhurried
coffee or lunch in Harvard
Square. Also in the North
End (255 Hanover Street).
✚ C3 ✉ 1 Eliot Square
☎ 617/868–3240
🚇 Harvard Square

CAFFÈ VITTORIA
Popular North End spot
for an after-dinner coffee,
pastry, or gelato.

✚ d11; H4 ✉ 296 Hanover
Street ☎ 617/227–7606
🚇 Haymarket

HI-RISE BREAD COMPANY
Alfresco coffee and good
pastries in Harvard
Square's Blacksmith
House. Built 1811, this was
Henry W. Longfellow's
"Village Blacksmith."
✚ C2 ✉ 56 Brattle Street,
Cambridge ☎ 617/492–3003
🚇 Harvard Square

L.A. BURDICK CHOCOLATES
If heaven were a chocolate
shop it might look
something like this
Harvard Square café, which
serves coffee and decadent
chocolates.
✚ C2 ✉ 52 Brattle Street,
Cambridge ☎ 617/491–4340;
www.burdickchocolate.com
🚇 Harvard

TO GO BAKERY
South End locals line up
for the muffins, scones,
and cream cheese cake.
✚ F7 ✉ 314 Shawmut
Avenue ☎ 617/482–1015
⊙ Mon–Fri from 6.30AM; Sat
from 7; Sun from 8 🚇 Back Bay

A SPECIAL TEA

THE BRISTOL (FOUR SEASONS HOTEL)
Traditional high tea daily
at 3–4.30 (➤ 71).

MUSEUM OF FINE ARTS
Tea and music in the
Ladies' Committee Room.
✚ E6 ✉ 465 Huntington
Avenue, Fenway
☎ 617/267–9300;
www.mfa.org ⊙ Tue–Fri
2.30–4 🚇 Museum

TEALUXE

Few tables and a small selection of pastries, but plenty of tea choices—their motto is "Over 140 teas and one coffee." Also at 108 Newbury Street.
✚ C3 ⊠ Zero Brattle Street, Cambridge ☎ 617/441-0077; www.tealuxe.com 🕐 Mon–Sat 8AM–11PM; Sun 8AM–10PM 🚇 Harvard

LATE EATING

Bostonians generally eat early. For late eating, try Chinatown or:

BOMBOA ($$–$$$)

Don't let the trendy bar crowd keep you from finding a table here, where the Back Bay meets the South End. A creative mix of French and Brazilian, the dishes—ceviche, feijoada, or steak frites with *chimichurri* sauce—are eclectic and very good.
✚ G5 ⊠ 35 Stanhope Street ☎ 617/236-6363 🕐 Tue–Sat 5.30PM–midnight; Sun, Mon 5.30PM–10PM 🚇 Back Bay

THE BRISTOL (FOUR SEASONS HOTEL) ($$)

Gorge on calorific desserts in the Viennese Dessert Buffet by the fire or overlooking the Public Garden. Also late dining.
✚ G5 ⊠ 200 Boylston Street ☎ 617/338-4400 🕐 Sun–Thu 11AM–11.30PM; Fri, Sat 11AM–12.30AM. Viennese Dessert Buffet Fri, Sat 9PM–midnight 🚇 Arlington

CHEERS (BULL & FINCH PUB) ($)

Made famous by the popular TV series. Bar food served until late.

✚ alV; G5 ⊠ 84 Beacon Street ☎ 617/227-9605; www.cheersboston.com 🕐 Daily 11AM–1.30AM 🚇 Arlington

FINALE ($–$$)

Tucked behind the Four Seasons Hotel, serves light meals and elaborate desserts. Popular pre- and post-theatre. Try the $30 Chocolate Plate for Two.
✚ G5 ⊠ 15 Columbus Avenue, Theater District ☎ 617/423-3184 🕐 Mon–Fri lunch; dinner Mon until 10; Tue, Wed, Sun until 11; Thu–Sat until 12 🚇 Arlington

JUMBO SEAFOOD ($)

A crowded, no-decor Chinatown eatery serving first-rate Hong Kong-style seafood until the wee hours.
✚ H5 ⊠ 7 Hudson Street ☎ 617/542-2823 🕐 Sun–Wed till 1AM; Thu–Sat till 3AM 🚇 Chinatown

SONSIE ($$)

Hip haunt. Eclectic menu ranges from Vietnamese spring rolls to grilled vanilla-cured pork loin.
✚ F5 ⊠ 327 Newbury Street, Back Bay ☎ 617/351-2500; www.sonsieboston.com 🕐 7AM–midnight (Sun, Mon till 11) 🚇 Hynes/ICA

SOUTH STREET DINER ($)

Classic hole-in-the-wall diner in the Leather District; eggs, burgers, and coffee served at all hours.
✚ H5 ⊠ 178 Kneeland Street ☎ 617/350-0028 🕐 7PM–2PM 🚇 South Station

Also try: Top of the Hub (▶ 67) and Border Café (▶ 68).

ICE CREAM

Superb ice cream in Boston can be found at Emack & Bolio (⊠ 290 Newbury Street ☎ 617/247-8772), an ice cream, yogurt, and juice bar, who claim to have invented the sublime cookies-and-cream ice cream.

Steve's and Herrell's premium ice creams are both named after local ice cream wizard Steve Herrell (⊠ Faneuil Hall Marketplace ☎ 617/367-0569; ⊠ 15 Dunster Street, Harvard Square, Cambridge ☎ 617/497-2179).

J.P. Licks is also on Newbury Street (☎ 617/236-1666), as is Ben and Jerry's (⊠ 174 Newbury Street ☎ 617/536-5456), which has a shop in Harvard Square as well (⊠ 36 J.F.K. Street ☎ 617/864-2828).

Toscanini's, a local premium ice-cream shop, has a branch in Harvard Square (⊠ 1310 Massachusetts Avenue, Cambridge ☎ 617/354-9350).

Districts & Department Stores

There are several clearly defined shopping areas in Boston, each with its own personality. If you have time for only one spree, choose Newbury Street, which has to be one of the most beautiful streets for shoppers in the country.

ART GALLERIES

Newbury Street is the place to go if you are interested in buying artwork—paintings, prints, or sculpture. Many a pleasant hour can be spent browsing in the galleries here, stopping off in a café now and then. A concentration of them can be found between Arlington and Exeter streets. They display works by 18th- and 19th-century artists, in addition to contemporary pieces. Those interested in avant-garde galleries may like to explore the South End, particularly around Harrison/Thayer streets, where new galleries are popping up to join cooperatives such as Broomfield Art Gallery, at 11 Thayer Street, and the South of Washington Gallery, on the district's eastern (and still slightly rough-at-the-edges) periphery.

NEWBURY STREET

Running west from the Public Garden to Massachusetts Avenue through the Back Bay, Newbury Street's Victorian houses make a colourful corridor of enticing shops, galleries, and restaurants. Everything is here, from designer boutiques to secondhand clothes shops, from prestigious galleries to Virgin Megastore, from Giorgio Armani to small independents, from outdoor cafés to elegant restaurants. The east end of the street is the chic end.
✚ F5 🚇 Arlington, Copley, Hynes/ICA

CHARLES STREET

This is another delightful street of shops and restaurants, running north from the Public Garden through the flat area of Beacon Hill. It specializes in antique shops but has several gift shops and galleries too, and a selection of places where you can get a bite to eat.
✚ aIV; G4 🚇 Arlington, Charles

DOWNTOWN CROSSING

Shops selling street fashion, shoes, jewellery, cameras, and the like, plus the city's main department stores—and the legendary bargain hunters' mecca,

Filene's Basement (► 74). Encompassing part of Washington, Winter, and Bromfield streets, Downtown Crossing is mainly pedestrians-only.
✚ cIV; H5 🚇 Downtown Crossing

FANEUIL HALL MARKETPLACE

Souvenirs and New England crafts keep company with fashion, accessories, pewter, household-ware stores, a BosTix ticket agency booth (► 82), and plenty of eating options—all in and around three well-restored wharf buildings.
✚ dIII; H4 🚇 State

HARVARD SQUARE

Cambridge's Harvard Square is a maze of streets with dozens of bookshops (many stay open all evening), music shops, and clothes shops—new and secondhand—much of it geared to students. It's an entertaining place too, with a wide variety of restaurants and cafés. Check out Brattle Street, Church Street, Eliot Street (with the Charles Square complex just off), John F. Kennedy Street, and Dunster Street. As some of the chains have moved into the area, so some of the smaller local shops have moved, or opened up, just north of Harvard, and there's now a clutch of funky clothes and gift shops on Massachusetts Avenue heading towards Porter Square.
✚ C2–C3 🚇 Harvard Square

PRUDENTIAL CENTER AND COPLEY PLACE

A vast undercover complex in the Back Bay that encompasses two malls (► below), several hotels, and the Hynes Convention Center.

MALLS

CAMBRIDGESIDE GALLERIA

Scores of stores on three levels, some of which will appeal to the younger generation. Fashion outlets include Banana Republic, The Limited, J. Crew, Original Levi's Store, and Talbots. There are several footwear places (such as Nine West and Overland), music shops, a Disney store, pushcarts, eateries, and branches of the department stores Filene's and Sears.

✚ F3 ✉ 100 CambridgeSide Place 🕐 Mon–Sat 10–9.30; Sun 11–7 🚇 Lechmere or Kendall Square; free shuttle bus

CHESTNUT HILL

Mall at Chestnut Hill for stylish shopping in a classy suburb.

✚ Off map at A7 ✉ Hammond Pond Parkway, Chestnut Hill 🚇 Chestnut Hill then 15 minute walk

COPLEY PLACE

Copley is more refined than "the Pru" (the Prudential Center), to which it is connected by a covered bridge over Huntington Avenue. Elegant stores such as Tiffany's and Neiman-Marcus jostle with national chains and outlets for trendy kitchenware, high-tech gadgets, and very good crafts. There is a movie complex.

✚ F6 ✉ Huntington Avenue 🕐 Mon–Sat 10–7; Sun noon–6 🚇 Copley

PRUDENTIAL CENTER

A dozen clothes stores (including Ann Taylor, Chico's, Claiborne Men, Structure, and Original Levi's), some shoe and accessories shops, gift and specialty (such as stationery) stores, and a hardware store.

Also home to department stores Saks Fifth Avenue and Lord & Taylor, a post office, ATMs, Movenpick's superb food court, and Legal Sea Foods.

✚ F5–F6 ✉ Between Boylston Street and Huntington Avenue 🕐 Mon–Sat 10–8; Sun 11–6 🚇 Prudential

DEPARTMENT STORES

Two major department stores face each other in Downtown Crossing: Macy's, the bigger, and Filene's. Underneath Filene's is Filene's Basement (► 74). Other stores have branches in malls (► above). In Harvard Square there is The Coop, or the Harvard Cooperative Society. Strong on books and posters, it was started as a non-profit store for students in 1882 and is now the biggest department store in the centre of Cambridge.

OUTLET SHOPPING

Factory outlet shopping is now one of New England's biggest draws for visitors. The major outlet centres are out of Boston, but not more than an hour away. A whole range of merchandise—clothes, shoes, household and electrical goods, luggage—is discounted, sometimes as much as 65 percent off the normal retail price. All the well-known brand names keep cropping up, including Levi's, Calvin Klein, Liz Claiborne, Van Heusen, Ralph Lauren, Donna Karan, Bally, Timberland, Tommy Hilfiger, Hugo Boss, and Eddie Bauer.

Wrentham

Wide range of designer fashion outlets, 50 minutes southwest, off Route 495. The Back Bay coach will pick you up from your hotel (☎ 877/ 404–9909).

Worcester Common

More than 90 well-known designer and manufacturer stores, one hour west by Peter Pan bus from South Station (daily 9AM, returning 4PM) or by car on Route 1/90.

Fall River

Particularly known for linens, kitchenware, and furniture. One hour south of Boston.

Kittery

In Maine. Has more than 100 stores and is about an hour north on Route 95.

Freeport

Also in Maine, north of Kittery—the birthplace of outlet shopping, and home of outdoor clothing specialist L. L. Bean.

Clothes

JEWELLERY

John Lewis Inc
The stylish, contemporary jewellery displayed here is handcrafted from solid metal and semi-precious stones in a local studio.
✚ F5 ✉ 97 Newbury Street
☎ 617/266–6665
Ⓜ Arlington

Shreve, Crump & Low
This is *the* place to buy your diamonds, rubies, silver, and gold. Aside from anything else, it is a landmark building of the art deco period–just take a look at the silvered ceiling inside.
✚ G5 ✉ 330 Boylston Street
☎ 617/267–9100
Ⓜ Arlington

THE CHAIN

Most of the major American clothes chains are represented in Boston: Abercrombie & Fitch (Faneuil Hall Marketplace), Banana Republic (CambridgeSide Galleria, Newbury Street), French Connection, Gap, Giorgio Armani (Newbury Street), The Limited (Copley Place), Original Levi's (Prudential Center). British visitors will find familiar fashions at cheaper prices than back home.

NEW CLOTHES

ALAN BILZERIAN
A fun one for window shopping (or buying, of course, if you're very rich or very outrageous) for little numbers from Jean-Paul Gaultier, Katharine Hamnett, and the like.
✚ G5 ✉ 34 Newbury Street
☎ 617/536–1001
Ⓜ Arlington

ALLSTON BEAT
Funky gear for the supercool at the funky, supercool end of Newbury Street. Names like Doc Marten, Converse, Stussy, and Lip Service.
✚ E5 ✉ 348 Newbury Street
☎ 617/254–4420
Ⓜ Hynes/ICA

BELLE DE JOUR
The ultimate in silk, satin, and lace lingerie. There's help for men buying gifts.
✚ F5 ✉ 164 Newbury Street
☎ 617/236–4554 Ⓜ Copley

BETSEY JOHNSON
Pretty things in natural fabrics but with a touch of glamour for a special occasion, and locally knitted sweaters.
✚ F5 ✉ 201 Newbury Street
☎ 617/236–7072 Ⓜ Copley

CHICO'S
Comfortable and casual but stylish and affordable women's clothes, just that little bit different. Separates in natural fibres, as well as unusual jewellery and belts.
✚ F6 ✉ Prudential Center
☎ 617/247–3771
Ⓜ Prudential

CLOTHWARE
Contemporary women's clothing, including lots of knits and linens. Also lingerie and wacky hats.
✚ C2 ✉ 52 Brattle Street
☎ 617/261–6441
Ⓜ Harvard

EILEEN FISHER
Natural fabrics in elegant, simple designs for women's smart, casual day, and evening wear. The clothes come in a rich colour range.
✚ F6 ✉ Copley Place
☎ 617/536–6800
Ⓜ Copley

EMPORIO ARMANI
Slightly less haute couture but more accessible price-wise than Giorgio Armani (No. 22 Newbury Street). The store has a popular café, with outside tables in summer.
✚ G5 ✉ 210 Newbury Street
☎ 617/262–7300
Ⓜ Copley

FILENE'S BASEMENT
A Boston institution, this is the original bargain basement, beneath Filene's department store but separately managed. When a manufacturer or store has overstock (or goes under) the goods end up here and are offered at vastly discounted prices. The price is then marked down again and again until sold. The Basement gets incredibly crowded, so avoid lunchtime and weekends.
✚ clV; H5 ✉ Washington Street at Summer Street
☎ 617/642–2011
Ⓜ Downtown Crossing

JASMINE/SOLA/ SOLA MEN

Chic young designer clothes and shoes in Harvard Square (also 333 Newbury Street).

➕ C2 ✉ 37 Brattle Street
☎ 617/354–6043
🚇 Harvard

LOUIS BOSTON

High quality, expensive clothing for men and women in a spacious store just off Newbury Street. Nice café.

➕ G5 ✉ 234 Berkeley Street
☎ 617/262–6100
🚇 Arlington

PAVO REAL

Cotton, silk, and wool knitwear in rich (and subtle) colours and patterns. In Copley Place.

➕ F5 ✉ 100 Huntingdon Avenue ☎ 617/437–6699
🚇 Copley

RICCARDI

Dolce & Gabbana and other pricey Euro-chic labels for the young and the trendy.

➕ F5 ✉ 116 Newbury Street
☎ 617/266–3158 🚇 Copley

SERENDIPITY

Hip choice of ethnic designs from India, South America, and Africa.

➕ C3; F5 ✉ 1312 Massachusetts Avenue; 229 Newbury Street ☎ 617/661– 7143 🚇 Harvard; Copley

SIMON'S

Impeccable men's tailoring at this classic Proper Bostonian store in Copley Square. Alterations done on the premises.

➕ F5 ✉ 220 Clarendon Street
☎ 617/266–2345 🚇 Copley

STONESTREET

Stylish but expensive designer men's clothes. Business and business-casual.

➕ C2 ✉ 1276 Massachusetts Avenue ☎ 617/547–3245
🚇 Harvard

TALBOTS

Classic women's clothes for work or leisure. Neat suits and shirts, plus coats, casual wear, and night wear. Range of petite sizes.

➕ F5; H4 ✉ 500 Boylston Street; 25 School Street ☎ 617/ 262–2981 🚇 Copley; State

TESS

Stylish, classic clothes, shoes, and accessories for men and women.

➕ C3 ✉ 20 Brattle Street
☎ 617/846–8377
🚇 Harvard

URBAN OUTFITTERS

Where the young come to get that rugged look. Funky household goods.

➕ C3; F5 ✉ 11 J.F.K. Street/ Brattle Street; 321 Newbury Street ☎ 617/864–0070
🚇 Harvard; Hynes/ICA

SECONDHAND DESIGN

For that designer label you can't afford at a Newbury Street boutique.

THE CLOSET

Men and women's fashion.
➕ F5 ✉ 175 Newbury Street
☎ 617/536–1919 🚇 Copley

SECOND TIME AROUND

For women only. Also at 8 Eliot Street, Cambridge.
➕ F5 ✉ 167 Newbury Street
☎ 617/247–3504 🚇 Copley

CHILDREN'S CLOTHES

Calliope
For infants and young children up to size 6X. Largest selection of stuffed animals in Harvard Square; also baby toys.
✉ 33 Brattle Street
☎ 617/876–4149

Baby Gap/Gap Kids
Popular chain.
(Also in Copley Place, and at 15 Brattle Street, Harvard Square, in Cambridge.)
✉ 201 Newbury Street
☎ 617/424–8778

The Red Wagon
Brightly coloured, creatively casual T-shirt sets, dresses, and more for babies and young children. Cool kids' jewellery, too.
✉ 49 Charles Street
☎ 617/524–9402

Saturday's Child
Swank special-occasion (and expensive) outfits for infants, pre-schoolers, and kids. Many from European designers.
✉ 1762 Massachusetts Avenue ☎ 617/661–6402

Talbots Kids
Kids' branch of classic women's store (in the Prudential Center). Traditionally styled casual wear.
✉ 800 Boylston Street
☎ 617/266–9400

Shoes & Outdoor Gear

MORE CHOICE

These large outdoor activity stores are a little way out of the centre, all on Commonwealth Avenue.

Eastern Mountain Sports
Hiking, backpacking, camping, mountaineering, cross-country skiing. Also a smaller branch at 855 Boylston Street.
✉ 1041 Commonwealth Avenue ☎ 617/254–4250

Ski & Bike Market
Skiing, snowboarding, in-line skating, biking. Ski and snowboard rentals. Good children's section.
✉ 860 Commonwealth Avenue ☎ 617/731–6100

Wayland Golf Shop
Best names in clubs, bags, shoes, and more.
✉ 890 Commonwealth Avenue ☎ 617/277–3999

RENTING BICYCLES, IN-LINE SKATES, AND SKATEBOARDS

For bicycle hire, try Back Bay Bicycles.
✚ G5 ✉ 336 Newbury Street ☎ 617/247–2336
🚇 Hynes
Try Blades, Board & Skate (➤ this page) if you want to rent in-line skates and skateboards, or even have lessons. The shop has helpful staff.

SHOES

ALLEN EDMONDS
Top quality shoes in classic styles come in an impressively wide range of sizes.
✚ G5 ✉ 36 Newbury Street ☎ 617/247–3363
🚇 Arlington

FOOT PATHS
Elegant shoes for men and women, plus a full range of hiking boots. Also at 131 State Street.
✚ cIV; H5 ✉ 489 Washington Street ☎ 617/338–6008
🚇 Downtown Crossing

JOHN FLUEVOG
Classic or crazy, these Canadian designer's shoes for women deserve a look.
✚ F5 ✉ 302 Newbury Street ☎ 617/266–1079
🚇 Hynes/ICA

NIKETOWN
Large, state-of-the-art store, arranged by pavilion: men's and women's training and running, golf, basketball, soccer, tennis, and more.
✚ F5 ✉ 200 Newbury Street ☎ 617/267–3400
🚇 Copley

THE ROCKPORT STORE
The main outlet here for Rockport shoes and boots. Also at 83 Newbury Street. Stop by for a free bottle of water or a foot massage while you're checking out the shoes.
✚ dIII; H4 ✉ Faneuil Hall Marketplace ☎ 617/367–9996 🚇 State, Government Center

THE TANNERY
Wide range of hiking boots and sneakers (Vans, Timberland, Sebago, Rockport). Also in Brattle Street, Harvard Square.
✚ G5 ✉ 400 Boylston Street ☎ 617/267–0899
🚇 Arlington

OUTDOOR GEAR

BLADES, BOARD & SKATE
Good selection of board and skate gear. Also at 38 J.F.K. Street, Harvard Square, in Cambridge. Both do rentals and lessons.
✚ F5 ✉ 349a Newbury Street ☎ 617/437–6300
🚇 Hynes/ICA

DAKINI
Everything fleece for men, women, and children. Fleece boxer shorts, anyone? Designed more for urban style than rugged outdoor wear. Between Harvard and Porter squares.
✚ C1 ✉ 1704 Massachusetts Avenue ☎ 617/864–7661
🚇 Harvard, then walk or bus 77

HILTON'S TENT CITY
Good place for hiking and camping equipment, and performance clothing.
✚ cII; H4 ✉ 272 Friend Street ☎ 617/227–9242 🚇 North Station

PATAGONIA
The very best for stylish, efficient, comfortable outdoor gear. Irresistible. Plus all the latest camping and climbing equipment.
✚ F5 ✉ 346 Newbury Street ☎ 617/424–1776
🚇 Hynes/ICA

Books, Maps & Music

BOOKS & MAPS

Cambridge, and Harvard Square in particular, has an amazing concentration of independent bookshops; just a handful are mentioned here. Pick up a complete guide from the information kiosk by Harvard Square T. Chainstores such as Borders and Barnes & Noble are to be found throughout Boston and Cambridge.

AVENUE VICTOR HUGO
An institution. Huge collection of secondhand books on every subject.
➕ E5 ✉ 339 Newbury Street ☎ 617/266–7746 🚇 Hynes/ICA

BRATTLE BOOKSTORE
A treasure trove of rare and secondhand books with a good section on Boston and New England.
➕ bIV; G5 ✉ 9 West Street ☎ 617/542–0210 🚇 Park

GLOBE CORNER BOOKSTORE
Great for travel books and maps. Also at 28 Church Street, Cambridge.
➕ F5 ✉ 500 Boylston Street ☎ 617/859–8008 🚇 Copley

GROLIER POETRY BOOKSHOP
The US' only shop devoted entirely to poetry.
➕ C3 ✉ 6 Plympton Street, Cambridge ☎ 617/547–4648 🚇 Harvard

HARVARD BOOKSTORE
Known for academic titles and other kinds of non-fiction books. New titles and used books.
➕ C3 ✉ 1256 Massachusetts Avenue, Cambridge ☎ 617/661–1515 🚇 Harvard

RAND MCNALLY MAP & TRAVEL
Good range of maps and guides to New England—and elsewhere, too. Also at 800 Boylston Street.
➕ dIII; H4 ✉ 84 State Street ☎ 617/720–1125 🚇 State

WORDSWORTH
An absolute warren. Discounted prices.
➕ C3 ✉ 30 Brattle Street ☎ 617/354–5201 🚇 Harvard

MUSIC

In addition to Virgin Megastore (360 Newbury Street), HMV (1 Brattle Street, Cambridge), and Tower Records (249 Boylston Street, near Fenway Park), there is also the Borders books and music chain. More individual are:

CHEAPO RECORDS
Used rock, blues, and jazz albums, LPs, and 45s.
➕ D4 ✉ 645 Massachusetts Avenue, Cambridge ☎ 617/354–4455 🚇 Central

NEWBURY COMICS
The hippest record shop in town. Pop CDs plus T-shirts, posters, and comics. Also in Cambridge at 36 J.F.K. Street, and at the MIT Stratton Student Center, Massachusetts Avenue.
➕ F5 ✉ 332 Newbury Street ☎ 617/236–4930 🚇 Hynes/ICA

SHOPPING WITH/FOR CHILDREN

In Harvard Square:
Curious George goes to WordsWorth
WordsWorth's children's bookshop, full of delights.
✉ 1 J.F.K. Street ☎ 617/498–0062
Harvard Coop
A peaceful oasis of children's books is hidden in the store's basement. A calm, quiet place to browse—with or without the kids.
✉ 1400 Massachusetts Avenue ☎ 617/499–2000

In Faneuil Hall Marketplace:
Magic Hat is great for buying a trick or two—or just for watching the staff demonstrating them.
✉ Marketplace Center, Faneuil Hall Marketplace ☎ 617/439–8840

In Back Bay there is the toy emporium **FAO Schwarz**, with a giant teddy-bear sculpture outside.
✉ 440 Boylston Street ☎ 617/262–5900

Museums with particularly good shops for children are: the Children's Museum (► 61), the Museum of Fine Arts (► 30), the Museum of Science (► 36).

Crafts, Gifts & Household Goods

ANTIQUES

Charles Street
Pretty street at the foot of
Beacon Hill lined with a string
of 30 or so antiques shops
(mostly fairly pricey)—in
basements, on upper floors,
and down alleys; and there
are a few more in River Street.
Between them, you'll find
everything from 18th- and
19th-century European
furniture to porcelain, lighting,
linens, and garden furnishings.
🚇 Arlington, Charles

Cambridge
Cambridge has two
cooperatives, both with more
than 100 dealers selling china,
glass, quilts, clothes, silver,
jewellery, and collectables:
Cambridge Antique Market
✚ F3 ✉ 201 Monsignor
O'Brien Highway, diagonally
opposite Lechmere T ☎ 617/
868–9655 🚇 Lechmere
🔵 Closed Mon
**Antiques on Cambridge
Street**
✚ E3 ✉ 1076 Cambridge
Street (at Elm Street)
☎ 617/234–0001
🚇 Lechmere, then 69 bus
🔵 Closed Mon

CRAFTS

ALIANZA
Crafts, jewellery, and
teapots.
✚ F5 ✉ 154 Newbury Street
☎ 617/262–2385 🚇 Copley

ARTFUL HAND
American crafts, including
woven silk scarfs,
woodwork, ceramics, and
glass. In Copley Place
mall.
✚ F6 ✉ 36 Copley Place
☎ 617/262–9601 🚇 Copley,
Prudential

CAMBRIDGE ARTISTS'
COOPERATIVE
Quilts, weaving, jewellery,
scarves—all made locally.
✚ C2 ✉ 59a Church Street
☎ 617/868–4434
🚇 Harvard

MUSEUM OF FINE
ARTS
The museum shop has
contemporary ceramics,
jewellery, and silk scarves
(as well as books and
posters). Smaller shops in
several other locations.
✚ E6 ✉ 465 Huntington
Avenue ☎ 617/267–9300
🚇 Museum

SIGNATURE
Top American crafts in
wood, glass, ceramic, and
woven fabrics. On the
fringe of Faneuil.
✚ dIII; H4 ✉ 24 North Street
☎ 617/227–4885 🚇 State,
Government Center

SOCIETY OF
ARTS AND CRAFTS
Contemporary ceramics,
glass, woodwork, and
jewellery.
✚ F5 ✉ 175 Newbury Street
☎ 617/266–1810 🚇 Copley

GIFTS &
HOUSEHOLD
GOODS

For art ➤ 72, panel.

BLACK INK
An eclectic selection of
funky gifts and novelties:
shark staplers, alphabet
cookie cutters, bright
green frog banks,
architectural city guides.
✚ aIII; G4 ✉ 101 Charles
Street ☎ 617/723–3883
🚇 Charles, Arlington

BROMFIELD PEN SHOP
Pens, from vintage early
1900s models to new
Montblanc, Cross; and
cheap disposables.
✚ cIV; H4 ✉ 5 Bromfield
Street ☎ 617/482–9053
🚇 Park

BROOKSTONE
Hundreds of nifty little
gadgets. Also in Faneuil
Hall Marketplace.
✚ F6 ✉ Copley Place
☎ 617/267–4308 🚇 Copley

CRATE & BARREL
Well-designed, affordable
household goods:
Egyptian cotton sheets,
table linen, hand-blown
glass, kitchen utensils.
Also at 777 Boylston
Street, 48 Brattle Street,
and Copley Place.
✚ dIII; H4 ✉ Faneuil Hall
Marketplace
☎ 617/742–6025 🚇 State,
Government Center

EUGENE GALLERIES
Specializes in old maps
and prints, with a good
selection covering Boston.
✚ aIV; G4 ✉ 76 Charles
Street ☎ 617/227–3062
🚇 Charles

FRESH EGGS

"Everything for your nest"—or almost everything.

✚ G6 ✉ 58 Clarendon Street at Chandler Street ☎ 617/227-4646 🚇 Back Bay

HOUNDS ON THE HILL

Everything imaginable and more, for that dog or cat (or maybe its owner).

✚ alll; G4 ✉ 103 Charles Street ☎ 617/723-3266 🚇 Charles, Arlington

J. OLIVER'S

Crammed with tasteful and fun gifts.

✚ alV; G4 ✉ 38 Charles Street ☎ 617/723-3388 🚇 Charles, Arlington

LINENS ON THE HILL

Fine French linens—sheets, pillowcases, tablecloths. Also nightgowns and robes.

✚ alV; G4 ✉ 52 Charles Street ☎ 617/227-1255 🚇 Charles, Arlington

MDF

Modern Designer Furnishings: finely crafted picture frames, vases, serving pieces, lamps, and small tables.

✚ C3 ✉ 19 Brattle Street ☎ 617/491-2789 🚇 Harvard

MATSU

Chic gifts and (a few) clothes, many oriental.

✚ F5 ✉ 259 Newbury Street ☎ 617/266-9707 🚇 Copley, Hynes/ICA

NOSTALGIA FACTORY

Film posters (some vintage), old signs, advertisements, and more.

✚ dll; H4 ✉ 51 North Margin Street (off Salem Street) ☎ 617/720-2211 🚇 Haymarket

PIERRE DEUX

French fabrics, wallpapers, table linens, and lampshades.

✚ F5 ✉ 111 Newbury Street ☎ 617/536-6364 🚇 Arlington

RUGG ROAD PAPER

Handmade papers by the roll or sheet; paste papers, woodblocks, inks, ribbons, sealing wax, handbound albums and notebooks. Books (and classes) on paper-making and book binding.

✚ alll; G5 ✉ 105 Charles Street ☎ 617/742-0002 🚇 Charles, Arlington

SEASONINGS

Traditional cookware, French table linens, brushes of all sorts, kitchen utensils. Bridal registry.

✚ alll; G5 ✉ 113 Charles Street ☎ 617/227-2810 🚇 Charles, Arlington

STODDARD'S

Tiny shop packed to the gills with every conceivable type of knife and scissor.

✚ F6 ✉ Copley Place ☎ 617/536-8688 🚇 Copley

WILLIAMS-SONOMA

For the cook who has everything—or so you thought till you came in here: from Dualit toasters and heart-shaped muffin baking trays to French table linens and flour sack towels.

✚ F6 ✉ Copley Place ☎ 617/262-5892 🚇 Copley

FOOD

For New England specialties, wine, beers, and gourmet foods try: Cardullo's in Harvard Square (✉ 6 Brattle Street ☎ 617/491-8888). Explore the delis and *pasticcerias* of the Italian North End. Real food lovers can join a three-hour North End Market Tour, with specialist Michele Topor (☎ 617/523-6032 🕐 Wed, Sat 10AM, 2PM). For fruit and vegetables there's Boston's only street market, Blackstone Market—known as the "Haymarket"–near Faneuil Hall Marketplace (✉ Blackstone Street 🕐 Fri, Sat). Convenient if you're shopping in the Pru is Marché Movenpick, a groceries store within the mall (✉ Prudential Center at Huntington Avenue entrance). Pick up gourmet picnic foods from Savenor's (✉ 160 Charles Street ☎ 617/723-6328)–cheeses, patés, breads, fruits. At the other end of Charles Street (the Public Garden end) and also at 239 Newbury Street, is De Luca's Market, an excellent food store with some ready-made meals.

Classical Music, Opera & Dance

Star of the classical music scene is the Boston Symphony Orchestra (► Symphony Hall). Also worth considering are the many free performances such as those by the Boston Pops Orchestra.

CONCERT HALLS

BERKLEE PERFORMANCE CENTER

This Back Bay venue seats 1,220 and hosts jazz, pop, folk, and world music concerts by international performers and by the students and staff of the Berklee College of Music.
⊞ E6 ✉ 136 Massachusetts Avenue ☎ 617/266–7455, 617/747–2261; www.berkleebpc.com 🚇 Hynes/ICA

HATCH SHELL

The Boston Pops Orchestra gives free concerts here in early July. The highlight is the 4th of July concert, with fireworks. Locals come with a picnic. Other musical groups perform throughout the summer.
⊞ G4 ✉ Esplanade, Embankment Road ☎ 617/727–9547 ext.455; www.state.ma.us/mdc 🚇 Charles, Arlington

JORDAN HALL

This glittering and acoustically perfect venue, in the prestigious New England Conservatory, showcases the resident Boston Philharmonic, Boston Baroque, Cantata Singers, and Boston Gay Men's Chorus. Conservatory students perform free concerts year round.
⊞ F6 ✉ 30 Gainsborough Street, one block west of Symphony Hall ☎ 617/536–2412; www.newengland conservatory.edu/jordanhall/about.html 🚇 Symphony

SANDERS THEATRE

A 1,200-seat neo-Gothic theatre at Harvard, with classical and world music.
⊞ C2 ✉ Quincy Street at Cambridge Street, Cambridge ☎ 617/496–2222; www.fas.harvard.edu/~memhall/sanders.html 🚇 Harvard Square

SYMPHONY HALL

"Symphony" is home of the renowned Boston Symphony Orchestra from October to April. The orchestra performs on Friday afternoons, Saturday, Tuesday, and Thursday evenings. Open rehearsals are held some Wednesday evenings and Thursday mornings. The Boston Pops Orchestra concerts (started in 1885) are held here in May and June before moving to the Hatch Shell (► above) in July.
⊞ F6 ✉ 301 Massachusetts Avenue ☎ 617/266–1200 (box office); 617/266–1492 (general information); www.bso.org 🚇 Symphony

TSAI PERFORMANCE CENTER AT BOSTON UNIVERSITY

Students show off their musical talents, in free concerts. Also professional music and dance groups, as well as Boston University faculty recitals.
⊞ D5 ✉ 685 Commonwealth Avenue ☎ 617/353–6467; www.bu.edu/tsai 🚇 Boston University East

CHORAL AND EARLY MUSIC GROUPS

Boston has more than its fair share of choirs and early music groups, including the oldest music organization in the US, the Handel & Haydn Society (☎ 617/266–3605; www.handelandhaydn.org)– established in 1815 and still performing regularly at Symphony Hall and Jordan Hall. Other groups to look for are Boston Camerata (☎ 617/262–2092), for medieval music; Chorus Pro Musica (☎ 617/267–7442; www.choruspromusica.org), for choral music from the Renaissance to the present; and the Cantata Singers (☎ 617/267–6502)–based at Jordan Hall–for Bach to contemporary works.

SMALLER VENUES & CHAMBER MUSIC

EMMANUEL CHURCH

A Bach cantata every
Sunday (September to
May).
⊞ G5 ✉ 15 Newbury Street
☎ 617/536–3356;
www.emmanuelmusic.org
Ⓜ Arlington

ISABELLA STEWART GARDNER MUSEUM

The great arts patron
began hosting chamber
concerts in her Venetian-
style mansion (➤ 29), and
the museum still runs
concerts here on weekends
(September to May).
⊞ D6 ✉ 280 The Fenway
☎ 617/566–1401;
www.gardnermuseum.org
Ⓜ Museum

KING'S CHAPEL

Free concerts Tuesdays
(12.15); vocal and organ
recitals.
⊞ H4 ✉ 58 Tremont Street
☎ 617/523–1749; www.kings-
chapel.org Ⓜ Park,
Government Center

MUSEUM OF FINE ARTS

Baroque chamber concerts
by the Boston Museum
Trio and others, in the
Remis Auditorium
on Sunday afternoons
(September to May), jazz
concerts in the courtyard
on Wednesday evenings in
summer (➤ 30).
⊞ E6 ✉ 465 Huntington
Avenue ☎ 617/267–9300;
www.mfa.org Ⓜ Museum

TRINITY CHURCH

This landmark (➤ 34)
makes a super backdrop
for free organ and choir
recitals, Fridays (12.15).

⊞ F5 ✉ Copley Square
☎ 617/536–0944; www.trinity
churchboston.org Ⓜ Copley

OPERA & DANCE

BALLET THEATER OF BOSTON

Directed by José Mateo,
this notable professional
company performs a
community-friendly mix
of classical and
contemporary ballet.
⊞ C3 ✉ 400 Harvard Street,
Cambridge ☎ 617/354–7467;
www.btb.org Ⓜ Harvard

BOSTON BALLET

➤ Wang Center, below.

BOSTON LYRIC OPERA

A fast-growing opera
company that performs
several productions each
season at the Shubert
Theater (➤ 83).
✉ 45 Franklin Street (company
offices) ☎ 617/542–6772;
www.blo.org

EMERSON MAJESTIC THEATER

Visiting dance troupes,
world music performers,
Shakespearean actors, and
Emerson College student
productions all use the
stage at this 1903 venue.
⊞ G5 ✉ 219 Tremont Street
☎ 617/824–8000;
www.maj.org Ⓜ Boylston

WANG CENTER FOR PERFORMING ARTS

A 1920s movie palace used
for concerts, opera, dance,
and the impressive Boston
Ballet (☎ 617/695–6950),
which performs classical
and contemporary dance.
⊞ G5 ✉ 270 Tremont Street;
www.wangcenter.org ☎ 617/
482–9393 Ⓜ Boylston

ALTERNATIVE DANCE

Contemporary and ethnic
dance troupes perform at
venues all over the city and
beyond.
In Boston, these include the
Dance Collective
(☎ 781/861–0735;
www.dancecollective.org) and
Art of Black Dance and Music
(☎ 617/666–1859;
www.abdm.net).
In Cambridge, look for the
Multicultural Arts Center
(✉ 41 2nd Street
☎ 617/577–1400;
www.cmacusa.org), and the
Dance Complex (✉ 536
Massachusetts Avenue
☎ 617/547–9363;
www.dancecomplex.org).
In spring, a series of
performances and workshops
is held every year by the 30-
member Mandala Folk Dance
Ensemble (☎ 617/868–3641;
www.ultranet.com/~mandala).

Theatre & Cinema

Boston, once regarded as something of a theatrical backwater, has now a proliferation of fringe, student, and innovative companies, adding spice to the mainstream fare. There is also a wide choice of cinemas showing alternative films.

THEATRE

AMERICAN REPERTORY THEATER

A highly regarded professional repertory company based in Harvard Square, staging classical and original drama.

✚ C2 ✉ Loeb Drama Center, 64 Brattle Street, Cambridge ☎ 617/547–8300; www. amrep.org 🚇 Harvard Square

BOSTON CENTER FOR THE ARTS

Three stages at this South End performance space house several contemporary theatre companies, including the Irish-themed Súgán Theatre and the cutting-edge SpeakEasy Stage Company.

✚ G6 ✉ 539 Tremont Street ☎ 617/426–7700; www.bcaonline.org 🚇 Back Bay

CHARLES PLAYHOUSE

Shear Madness, a comedy whodunnit set in a hairdresser's, has played here since 1980. *Blue Man Group*, another long-running show, presents its offbeat mix of theatre, music, and performance art on the Charles' other stage.

✚ G5 ✉ 74 Warrenton Street ☎ 617/426–5225 (*Shear Madness*); 617/426–6912 (*Blue Man Group*) 🚇 Boylston

COLONIAL THEATER

This lush, beautifully restored, turn-of-the-19th-century theatre stages pre-Broadway productions as well as a range of other performing arts events.

✚ G5 ✉ 106 Boylston Street ☎ 617/426–9366; www.broadwayinboston.com 🚇 Boylston

EMERSON MAJESTIC THEATER (▶ 81)

HASTY PUDDING THEATER

Home to the touring Harvard's Hasty Pudding Theatricals company and to the American Repertory Theater's annual "New Stages" series of contemporary plays.

✚ C3 ✉ 12 Holyoke Street, Cambridge ☎ 617/495–5205; www.hastypudding.org 🚇 Harvard Square

HUNTINGTON THEATER COMPANY

From Boston University's resident professional troupe; includes European and American, classical and modern, comedies, and musicals.

✚ F6 ✉ 264 Huntington Avenue ☎ 617/266–0800; www.bu.edu/huntington 🚇 Symphony

LYRIC STAGE

This venue, on the second floor of the YWCA building, specializes in classics and new American shows.

✚ F5 ✉ 140 Clarendon Street ☎ 617/437–7172; www.lyric.stage.com 🚇 Back Bay

TICKETS

BosTix sell half-price theatre tickets on the day of the show (from 11AM). As a fully-fledged Ticketmaster outlet, it also sells full-price tickets in advance for venues in Boston and the rest of New England. Booths are at: ✉ Faneuil Hall Marketplace 🚇 Tue–Sat 10–6; Sun 11–4; ✉ Copley Square 🚇 Mon–Sat 10–6; Sun 11–4. Tickets cover theatre, concerts, museums, sports events, and trolley tours. All are sold for cash only.

PUPPET SHOWPLACE THEATER
Children—and adults—enjoy the puppetry here.
➕ C7 ✉ 32 Station Street, Brookline ☎ 617/731–6400; www.puppetshowplace.org
Ⓣ Brookline Village (green line D)

SHUBERT THEATER
An institution, founded in 1910, in the heart of the Theater District, which produces major pre- and post-Broadway shows.
➕ G5 ✉ 265 Tremont Street ☎ 617/482–9393 Ⓣ Boylston

WILBUR THEATER
Built in 1914, this stage hosts pre-Broadway and other touring shows.
➕ G5 ✉ 246 Tremont Street ☎ 617/423–4008; www.broadwayinboston.com
Ⓣ Boylston

CINEMA

BOSTON PUBLIC LIBRARY
The occasional film series usually features lesser-known old films.
➕ F5 ✉ Copley Square ☎ 617/536–5400; www.bpl.org Ⓣ Copley

BRATTLE THEATER
Vintage films and film festivals attract connoisseurs to this small, one-screen cinema.
➕ C3 ✉ 40 Brattle Street, Cambridge ☎ 617/876–6837; www.brattlefilm.org
Ⓣ Harvard Square

COOLIDGE CORNER THEATER
A fine art deco venue showing an intelligent selection of vintage and contemporary films.
➕ C6 ✉ 290 Harvard Street, Brookline ☎ 617/734–2501; www.coolidge.org Ⓣ Coolidge Corner (green line C)

HARVARD FILM ARCHIVE
Daily showings of cult and independent films at Harvard's Carpenter Center for the Visual Arts.
➕ C3 ✉ 24 Quincy Street, Cambridge ☎ 617/495–4700; www.harvardfilmarchive.org
Ⓣ Harvard Square

LANDMARK'S KENDALL SQUARE CINEMA
A multiscreen cinema also showing offbeat and foreign films. (There's a free shuttle bus every 20 minutes from Kendall station to CambridgeSide Galleria and the cinema.)
➕ F4 ✉ 1 Kendall Square, Cambridge ☎ 617/494–9800; www.landmarkstheatres.com
Ⓣ Kendall, then walk or bus

MUSEUM OF FINE ARTS
International, early, and offbeat films.
➕ E6 ✉ 465 Huntington Avenue ☎ 617/267–9300; www.mfa.org/film/ Ⓣ Museum

SONY/LOEWS THEATERS
The Harvard Square Theater shows mainstream, independent, and foreign films. The Loews Boston Common and Loews Copley Place show first-runs.
➕ C2 ✉ 10 Church Street, Cambridge ☎ 617/864–4580 Ⓣ Harvard; ➕ G5 ✉ 175 Tremont Street ☎ 617/423–3499 Ⓣ Boylston; ➕ F6 ✉ Copley Place ☎ 617/266–1300 Ⓣ Copley

A BIT OF VARIETY
Fans of old-time vaudeville might like to take a trip out of Boston to Beverly, where Le Grand David and His Own Spectacular Magic Company offer good old-fashioned entertainment at:
Cabot Street Cinema Theater
✉ 286 Cabot Street
☎ 978/927–3677
Ⓞ Most Suns
Larcom Theater
✉ 13 Wallis Street
☎ 978/927–3677
Ⓞ Occasional Sats

Clubs & Bars

WATERFRONT CONCERTS

Summer pop concerts are held in the FleetBoston Pavilion on Fan Pier (✉ 290 Northern Avenue ☎ 617/728–1600). Tickets are expensive, but with the views of the downtown skyline, you may not mind.

QUIETER CHOICES

If you'd rather hear yourself think than groove the night away, check out Boston's hotel lounge bars—many with low-key music, some with food. Try the Oak Bar, in the glittering Fairmont Copley Plaza Hotel, Copley Square (➤ 86); the Bristol Lounge in the Four Seasons Hotel (➤ 71), where classical piano or jazz music accompanies the sublime Viennese Dessert Buffet; the Atrium Lounge at the Millennium Bostonian Hotel, Faneuil Hall, where a pianist performs Friday and Saturday evenings.
See also the Regattabar and Scullers entries.

JAZZ, BLUES & FOLK

CLUB PASSIM
The area's premier folk music venue attracts both up-and-coming and well-established performers.
➕ C2 ✉ 47 Palmer Street, Cambridge ☎ 617/492–7679; www.clubpassim.com
🔵 Harvard

HOUSE OF BLUES
The Harvard Square branch of this national chain features live music and a very popular Sunday gospel group brunch.
➕ C3 ✉ 96 Winthrop Street, Cambridge ☎ 617/491–2583; www.hob.com 🔵 Live shows from 9PM Sun–Wed; from 10PM Thu–Sat 🔵 Harvard

JOHNNY D'S UPTOWN
Good light meals and fine sounds, including blues and world music in Somerville's Davis Square, just north of Cambridge. Frequent performances by zydeco and Latin groups.
➕ Off map at 1C
✉ 17 Holland Street, Somerville ☎ 617/776–2004; www.johnnyds.com 🔵 Music Tue–Sun 🔵 Davis Square

REGATTABAR
First-class jazz acts come to Harvard Square at this classy bar in the Charles Hotel.
➕ C3 ✉ 1 Bennett Street, Cambridge ☎ 617/864–1200, 617/876–7777; www.concertix.com 🔵 Closed Mon 🔵 Harvard Square

RYLES
Another Cambridge hotspot, in Inman Square, with food downstairs. Emphasis now on Latin jazz. Weekly learn-to-salsa Latin dance night.
➕ D3 ✉ 212 Hampshire Street, Cambridge ☎ 617/876–9330; www.rylesjazz.com 🔵 Music Tue–Sun from 8.30PM; Sun brunch 10–3 🔵 Central then long walk or bus 83; Harvard then bus 69 along Cambridge Street

SCULLERS
Famous names perform smooth jazz in this bar at the Doubletree Suites Hotel, Tuesday to Saturday (and some Sundays). Reserve in advance.
➕ C4 ✉ 400 Soldiers Field Road at River Street Bridge ☎ 617/562–4111; www.scullersjazz.com

MUSIC & DANCE CLUBS

AVALON
Combining live acts and dance, this Lansdowne Street megaclub offers International on Thursday, "Avaland" night with top DJs on Friday, mainstream on Saturday, and gay night on Sunday.
➕ E5 ✉ 15 Lansdowne Street ☎ 617/262–2424; www.avalonboston.com 🔵 Thu–Sun 10PM–2PM 🔵 Kenmore

AXIS
Next door to Avalon, Axis features live bands playing house, soul, funk, and alternative music.
➕ E5 ✉ 13 Lansdowne Street ☎ 617/262–2437; www.axisnightclub.com 🔵 Thu–Sat 10PM–2AM 🔵 Kenmore

KARMA CLUB
DJs and live music.
🚇 E5 ✉ 9 Lansdowne Street
☎ 617/421–9595 🕐 Thu
9PM–2AM; Fri, Sat 10PM–2AM
🚇 Kenmore

RHYTHM & SPICE CARIBBEAN BAR & GRILL
A restaurant/club near MIT that attracts a multiracial mix of students and professionals. After sampling Jamaican jerk chicken, curried goat, or rotis, stay for reggae, soca, and other island rhythms.
🚇 E4 ✉ 315 Massachusetts Avenue (Main Street) ☎ 617/497–0977; www.rspice.com
🕐 Music Thu 10.30PM–2AM; Fri, Sat 11PM–2AM; Sun 10.30PM–1AM
🚇 Central, then walk

THE ROXY
One of the city's largest nightclubs plays Latin music Thursdays, International house Fridays, and American house Saturdays.
🚇 G5 ✉ 279 Tremont Street
☎ 617/338–7699;
www.roxyboston.com 🕐 Thu 10PM–2AM; Fri 10.30PM–2AM; Sat 9PM–2AM 🚇 Boylston

BARS, COMEDY & GAMES

BOSTON BILLIARD CLUB
Popular Fenway Park hangout for pool addicts.
🚇 D6 ✉ 126 Brookline Avenue ☎ 617/536–POOL; www.bostonbilliardclub.com
🕐 Noon–2AM 🚇 Kenmore

COMEDY CONNECTION
A first-class comedy club, with shows every night. Reserve ahead.
🚇 dIII; H4 ✉ Faneuil Hall Marketplace ☎ 617/248–9700; www.comedyconnection boston.com 🕐 Shows Mon–Wed 8PM; Thu 8.30PM; Fri, Sat 8, 10.15PM; Sun 7PM 🚇 State, Government Center

DICK DOHERTY'S COMEDY VAULT
A leading comedy club, in a former bank vault.
🚇 G5 ✉ 124 Boylston Street
☎ 617/482–0110;
www.dickdoherty.com 🕐 Shows Thu–Sun 🚇 Boylston

IMPROV ASYLUM
Improvisational comedy at a North End cabaret-style theatre and in a larger Theater District club.
🚇 dII; H4 ✉ 216 Hanover Street ☎ 617/263–6887; www.improvasylum.com
🕐 Shows Wed–Sat
🚇 Haymarket; 🚇 G5 ✉ 75 Warrenton Street ☎ 617/263–6887; www.improvasylum.com
🕐 Shows Wed–Sun 🚇 Boylston

JILLIAN'S
Virtual sports, 200 high-tech games, 50 pool tables, plus five bars and bistro-style food.
🚇 E6 ✉ 145 Ipswich Street
☎ 617/437–0300;
www.jilliansboston.com 🕐 Pool Hall Mon–Sat 11AM–2AM; Sun noon–2AM. Games Mon–Fri 3PM–2AM; Sat 11AM–2AM; Sun noon–2AM 🚇 Kenmore

NICK'S COMEDY STOP
A well-loved Theater District comedy club with local stars and would-be stars on stage.
🚇 G5 ✉ 100 Warrenton Street ☎ 617/482–0930; www.nickscomedystop.com
🕐 Shows generally Thu 8.30; Fri, Sat 8.45 🚇 Boylston

NIGHTLIFE AND CRUISES

Odyssey
Operates evening cruises on a 600-passenger yacht, plus a Sunday jazz brunch and weekday lunches (advanced reservations required).
✉ Atlantic Avenue; sails from Rowes Wharf
☎ 617/654–9710 or 800/946–7245; www.odyssey cruises.com/boston

The Spirit of Boston
Has live bands and shows on its dinner dance cruises.
✉ Northern Avenue; sails from World Trade Center
☎ 617/748–1450; www.spirit cruises.com
🕐 Lunch and dinner cruises daily in season

Luxury Hotels

PRICES

For a standard double room in a luxury hotel expect to pay from $150–$435 (off-season) to $355–$625 in peak season (► 4). However, with prices varying according to days of the week and the time of year, some hotel rates may lie in the mid-range category, opposite. For hotels in all price categories, always be sure to ask if there are any special deals: Some hotels offer winter rates and/or theatre weekends. If you have children, ask about family packages. Note also that many luxury and mid-range hotels have restaurants (► 64–65).

HEALTH AND FITNESS

Unless otherwise noted, all hotels listed on this page and on the mid-range page either have fitness centres and pools within the hotel, or offer use of nearby health spas (sometimes there is a fee to pay for these).

BUSINESS FACILITIES

The luxury and mid-range hotels listed here generally offer standard business facilities.

BOSTON HARBOR

Modern, elegant, 230-room hotel on the waterfront. It's worth paying a little more for harbour views. Good restaurant, with views.
🕂 eIV; J4 ✉ 70 Rowes Wharf ☎ 617/439–7000 or 800/752–7077; fax 617/345–6799; www.bhh.com 🚇 Aquarium

CHARLES

Modern 293-room hotel in Harvard Square. Home of Rialto, Henrietta's Table, and Regattabar jazz club.
🕂 C3 ✉ One Bennett Street, Cambridge ☎ 617/864–1200 or 800/882–1818; fax 617/864–5715; www.charleshotel.com 🚇 Harvard

COPLEY SQUARE

143-room hotel with European flavour. No fitness centre or pool.
🕂 F5 ✉ 47 Huntington Avenue, Back Bay ☎ 617/536–9000 or 800/225–7062; fax 617/267–3547; www.copleysquarehotel.com 🚇 Copley

FAIRMONT COPLEY PLAZA

A "grand dame" of Boston, with sumptuous decor (if you don't stay here, at least take a tour). 379 rooms.
🕂 F5 ✉ 138 St. James Avenue, Back Bay ☎ 617/267–5300 or 800/527–4727; fax 617/247–6681; www.fairmont.com 🚇 Copley

FOUR SEASONS

All you could ask for in elegance and service. Aujourd'hui and Bristol restaurants. 274 rooms.
🕂 G5 ✉ 200 Boylston Street, Back Bay ☎ 617/338–4400 or 800/332–3442; fax 617/423–0154; www.fourseasons.com/boston 🚇 Arlington

LE MERIDIEN

Historic 1920s building in the Financial District. 326 rooms. Julien restaurant.
🕂 dIV; H4 ✉ 250 Franklin Street ☎ 617/451–1900 or 800/543–4300; fax 617/423–2844; www.lemeridienboston.com 🚇 State, Downtown Crossing

LENOX

Built in 1900, this 212-room independent is one of the best.
🕂 F5 ✉ 710 Boylston Street ☎ 617/536–5300 or 800/225–7676, fax 617/267–1237; www.lenoxhotel.com 🚇 Copley

MILLENNIUM BOSTONIAN

This 201-room hotel is more intimate than some, and offers comfort without glitz. Seasons Restaurant.
🕂 dIII; H4 ✉ Faneuil Hall Marketplace ☎ 617/523–3600 or 866/866–8086; fax 617/523–2454; www.millennium-hotels.com 🚇 State, Government Center

WESTIN

Thirty-six floors, 800 handsome rooms, and direct access to Copley Place mall. Jazz nights in the Turner Fisheries Bar.
🕂 F5 ✉ 10 Huntington Avenue, Back Bay ☎ 617/262–9600 or 800/228–3000; fax 617/424–7483; www.starwood.com/westin/ 🚇 Copley

XV BEACON

Sixty-three chic rooms with all manner of electronics. Pampering service extends to the Federalist Restaurant.
🕂 H4 ✉ 15 Beacon Street ☎ 617/670–1500 or 877/982–3226; fax 617/670–6925 🚇 Park

Mid-Range Hotels

BACK BAY HILTON

Convenient to the Pru/Hynes centres. 385 rooms.
✚ F6 ✉ 40 Dalton Street, Back Bay ☎ 617/236–1100 or 800/874–0663; fax 617/867–6104; www.hilton.com
🚇 Prudential, Hynes/ICA

BEACON HILL HOTEL AND BISTRO

Thirteen tasteful, unfussy rooms in two linked townhouses. Lovely roof deck.
✚ G4 ✉ 25 Charles Street ☎ 617/723–7575 or 888/959–2442; fax 617/723–7525; www.beaconhillhotel.com
🚇 Charles

BOSTON PARK PLAZA

Elegant hotel built in 1927, with 972 rooms. Near the Public Garden and Theater District. Family friendly. Bonfire Restaurant, owned by Todd English.
✚ G5 ✉ 64 Arlington Street ☎ 617/426–2000 or 800/225–2008; fax 617/423–1708; www.bostonparkplaza.com
🚇 Arlington

COLONNADE

Behind the bland 1960s facade of this 285-room hotel near the Pru are traditionally decorated rooms. Rooftop pool. Home of Brasserie Jo.
✚ F6 ✉ 120 Huntington Avenue, Back Bay ☎ 617/424–7000 or 800/962–3030; fax 617/424–1717; www.colonnadehotel.com
🚇 Prudential

ELIOT

Elegance, comfort, and value. 95 suites with living room and kitchenette. Clio restaurant.
✚ E5 ✉ 370 Commonwealth Avenue, Back Bay ☎ 617/267–1607 or 800/44 ELIOT; fax 617/536–9114; www.eliothotel.com
🚇 Hynes/ICA

MARRIOTT COPLEY PLACE

A 38-floor, 1,147-room hotel in Copley Place mall. Covered walkway to Pru/Hynes. Good value winter deals.
✚ F6 ✉ 110 Huntington Avenue ☎ 617/236–5800 or 800/228–9290; fax 617/236–5885; www.marriott.com
🚇 Prudential, Copley

OMNI PARKER HOUSE

A rather staid 551-room, 19th-century hotel, near Boston Common. Chefs here invented two traditional American dishes—the Parker House roll and Boston cream pie.
✚ cIV; H4 ✉ 60 School Street, downtown ☎ 617/227–8600 or 800/843–6664; fax 617/742–5729; www.omniparkerhouse.com 🚇 Park

SHERATON BOSTON

1,200 rooms in two 29-floor towers, connected by interior walkways to the Pru and Hyne. Caters to business travellers, but family-friendly too.
✚ F6 ✉ Prudential Center, 39 Dalton Street ☎ 617/236–2000 or 800/325–3535; fax 617/236–1702; www.sheraton.com 🚇 Prudential, Hynes/ICA

SWISSÔTEL

The modern facade belies classic European elegance inside this 501-room hotel.
✚ cV; H5 ✉ 1 Avenue de Lafayette ☎ 617/451–2600 or 800/621–9200; fax 617/451–2198; www.swissotel.com
🚇 Downtown Crossing

PRICES

For a standard double room in a mid-range hotel, expect to pay from $130–$235 (off-season) to $260–$335 in peak season (▶ 4).

IN CAMBRIDGE

Mid-range options include:
Hyatt Regency
On the Charles river, with a revolving rooftop lounge. 479 rooms.
✉ 575 Memorial Drive ☎ 617/492–1234 or 800/233–1234; fax 617/491–6906; www.cambridge.hyatt.com
A Cambridge House
A Victorian bed & breakfast inn in north Cambridge. 15 rooms.
✉ 2218 Massachusetts Avenue ☎ 617/491–6300 or 800/232–9989; fax 617/868 2848; www.acambridgehouse.com 🚇 Porter
Mary Prentiss Inn
A 20-room antique-filled bed-and-breakfast with modern amenities.
✉ 6 Prentiss Street ☎ 617/661–2929; fax 617/661–5989; www.maryprentissinn.com 🚇 Porter

Budget Accommodation

PRICES

You should get a double room in the majority of the establishments listed here for under $100; expect to pay around $130–$200 in peak season (► 4).

BED & BREAKFAST AND ACCOMMODATION WITH COOKING FACILITIES

There is a shortage of characterful budget-priced hotels in Boston. As a pleasant alternative consider a bed & breakfast (many are in very comfortable private homes) or rooms with kitchenettes. Double occupancy in bed-and-breakfast accommodation ranges from $90–$180. Try: **Bed & Breakfast Agency of Boston** A helpful, friendly agency that will find you accommodation in historic houses and restored waterfront lofts. Nightly, weekly, monthly, and winter rates (✉ 47 Commercial Wharf ☎ 617/720–3540 or 800/248–9262; fax 617/523–5761; www.boston-bnbagency.com).

OUT OF TOWN

To reduce hotel costs, consider staying in Concord, Salem, or Rockport, all charming places that are 40-60 minutes from Boston and served by regular train services. For lodging suggestions, contact:
Concord Chamber of Commerce
✉ 978/369–3120, www.concordmachamber.org
Destination Salem
✉ 978/741-3252 or 877/725-3662; www.salem.org
Rockport Chamber of Commerce
✉ 978/546-6575; www.rockportusa.com

BEST WESTERN

Near medical complexes and Fenway Park. 160 rooms.
✚ D7 ✉ 342 Longwood Avenue ☎ 617/731–4700 or 800/528–1234; fax 617/731–6273; www.bestwestern.com 🚇 Green line D to Longwood

BOSTON INTERNATIONAL YOUTH HOSTEL

Dormitories; cooking facilities available. 205 beds.
✚ E6 ✉ 12 Hemenway Street ☎ 617/536–9455; fax 617/424–6558; www.bostonhostel.org 🚇 Hynes/ICA

CHANDLER INN

Inexpensive, basic 56-room hotel in the attractive South End. Gay-friendly. Short walk from Copley Square and Tremont Street restaurant row.
✚ G6 ✉ 26 Chandler Street ☎ 617/482–3450 or 800/842–3450; fax 617/542–3428; www.chandlerinn.com 🚇 Back Bay

HOLIDAY INN

A functional base at the foot of Beacon Hill's north slope. Outdoor pool. 303 rooms.
✚ bIII; G4 ✉ 5 Blossom Street ☎ 617/742–7630 or 800/HOLIDAY; fax 617/742–4192; www.holiday-inn.com 🚇 Charles, Bowdoin

HOWARD JOHNSON BOSTON BAYSIDE

Inexpensive option 5km (3 miles) south of town. Outdoor pool, bowling alley nearby. 133 rooms.
✚ Off map at H10 ✉ 900 Morrissey Boulevard, Dorchester ☎ 617/287–9200 or 800/446–4656; fax 617/282–2365; www.hojo.com 🚇 J.F.K., then half-hourly hotel shuttle bus 7AM–10PM

JOHN JEFFRIES HOUSE

Four-floor brick inn on Beacon Hill; 46 mostly tiny rooms. The two-room suites are better value.
✚ aIII; G4 ✉ 14 David Mugar Way (formerly Embankment Road) at Charles Circle ☎ 617/367–1866; fax 617/742–0313 🚇 Charles

NEWBURY GUEST HOUSE

Victorian-style rooms (32) in three connected redbrick row houses. Excellent value, popular; reserve well ahead.
✚ F5 ✉ 261 Newbury Street ☎ 617/437–7666 or 800/437–7668; fax 617/262–4243; www.hagopianhotels.com 🚇 Copley, Hynes/ICA

TREMONT BOSTON

Theater District 1920s hotel. Chandeliers in public areas, modern furnishings in the 323 bedrooms. Rates span the budget/mid-range categories.
✚ G5 ✉ 275 Tremont Street ☎ 617/426–1400 or 800/331–9998; fax 617/482–6730; www.wyndham.com/Tremont 🚇 Boylston

YMCA CENTRAL

Shared bathrooms—but maid service. In summer open to anyone over 18; in school year to men only. 90 rooms.
✚ E6 ✉ 316 Huntington Avenue ☎ 617/536–7800; fax 617/267–4653; www.ymcaboston.org 🚇 Green line E to Northeastern

BOSTON
travel facts

ESSENTIAL FACTS

Alcohol

- It is illegal to drink alcohol in public places such as the T.
- It is illegal to sell alcohol to anyone under the age of 21. Alcohol is not sold in shops on Sundays or after 11PM Monday to Saturday.

Customs regulations for visitors from outside the US

- Visitors aged 21 or more may import duty-free: 200 cigarettes, or 50 cigars, or 2kg of tobacco; 1 litre (1 US quart) of alcohol; and gifts up to $100 in value.
- It is forbidden to bring food, seeds, and plants into the US.
- Some medication bought over the counter abroad might be prescription-only in the US and may be confiscated. Bring a doctor's certificate for essential medication.

Electricity

- The US supply is 110 volts AC.
- US plugs have two pins.

Etiquette

- In restaurants a 5 percent meal tax is added to the bill. A tip of 15 to 20 percent is usually expected.
- Tip 15 percent for taxis and $1 to $1.50 a bag for hotel porters.
- Some restaurants require jackets and ties for men, but on the whole evening meals are informal affairs.
- Evening meals are usually served between 6 and 10PM on weekdays, later at weekends.

Money matters

- Nearly all banks have Automatic Teller Machines. Cards registered in other countries that are linked to the Cirrus or Plus networks are accepted. Before leaving, check which network your cards are linked to and ensure your PIN is valid in the US, where six-figure numbers are the norm.
- Credit cards are widely accepted.
- US dollar traveller's cheques function like cash in most places.
- Money and traveller's cheques can be exchanged at most banks (check commissions as they can be high) and many travel centres in central Boston.
- Some businesses may ask for photo identification before cashing traveller's cheques.

Opening hours

- Banks: Mon–Fri 9–3; Thu 9–5 or later; Sat 9–2.
- Shops: Mon–Sat 10–6 or later. Closed Sun mornings.
- Museums and sights: Unless otherwise stated, all sights mentioned in this book close on Thanksgiving and Christmas.
- Businesses: Mon–Fri 8 or 9–5.

Public Holidays

- 1 Jan (New Year's Day)
- 3rd Mon in Jan (Martin Luther King Day)
- 3rd Mon in Feb (President's Day)
- Last Mon in May (Memorial Day)
- 4th of July (Independence Day)
- 1st Mon in Sep (Labor Day)
- 2nd Mon in Oct (Columbus Day)
- 11 Nov (Veterans Day)
- 4th Thu in Nov (Thanksgiving)
- 25 Dec (Christmas Day)
- Boston also celebrates: 17 Mar (Evacuation Day); 3rd Mon in Apr (Patriots Day); 17 Jun (Bunker Hill Day).

Sensible precautions

- After dark, stick to well-lit and well populated areas. Avoid the lower half of Washington Street and Boston Common at night.

- Discuss your itinerary with your hotel's reception staff so they can point out any potential problems.
- Be aware of the people around you, especially at night or in quiet areas.
- Keep your wallet or purse out of sight and don't carry valuables or cash openly. Do not carry easily snatched bags and cameras, or put your wallet into your back pocket. In bars or restaurants, keep your belongings within reach.
- Keep valuables in your hotel's safe and never carry more money than you need.
- Lost traveller's cheques are relatively quick and easy to replace. Keep the numbers of the cheques separate from the cheques themselves.
- Report any stolen item to the nearest police station, if only to be able to claim on your insurance. The police will fill out the forms your insurance company will need.
- Always lock car doors and keep bags and valuables out of sight.

Smoking

- Smoking is banned in restaurants unless there is a separate seating area. It is banned in many public places, including the T. Some hotels have no-smoking floors.
- Cambridge is by law smoke-free.

Student travellers

- To get discounts on the T and admissions, get an International Student Identity Card (ISIC). If you are not a student but are under 26, get the International Youth Card (IYC).
- The Council on International Educational Exchange (CIEE) has a Travel Service offering domestic air passes for bargain travel within the US. It is also the exclusive agent for several student-discount cards (✉ 205 East 42nd Street, 16th Floor, New York, NY 10017 ☎ 800/268–6245 and in Boston ✉ 273 Newbury Street, Boston, MA 02116 ☎ 617/266–1926).
- Members of the Youth Hostel Association of England and Wales (✉ Trevelyan House, 8 St. Stephen's Hill, St. Albans, Herts, AL1 2DY ☎ 01727 855215) can use youth hostels.
- Information on student hostels within the US can be obtained from Hostelling International-American Youth Hostels ✉ 733 15th Street, Northwest, Suite 840, Washington, D.C. ☎ 202/783 6161 or 800/444 6111.

Telephones

- The area code for Boston and Cambridge is 617. This must be included even when making local calls. (New area codes are currently being introduced for new phone numbers).
- To call the US from the UK dial 00 1, followed by the area code and the number.
- To call the UK from the US, dial 011 44, then drop the initial zero from the area code.

Tickets

- The nine-day Boston CityPass (adult $30.25; seniors and youth discounts) gives half-price admission to six key sights: the Museum of Fine Arts, the Museum of Science, the New England Aquarium, the John F. Kennedy Library and Museum, Harvard Museum of Natural History, and Prudential Skywalk. Available from the above or at the visitor information centre on Boston Common or in the Prudential Center.
- For tickets for performing arts and sports events, museums, and trolley tours ► 82.

91

Time

- Massachusetts puts its clocks ahead one hour on the first Saturday in April until the last Saturday in October. (➤ 4 for more time information.)

Tourist offices

- Greater Boston Convention & Visitors Bureau Inc ✉ 2 Copley Place, Suite 105, Boston, MA 02116-6501 ☎ 617/536–4100; fax 617/424–7664; www.boston.usa.com.
- Massachusetts Office of Travel & Tourism ✉ State Transportation Building, 10 Park Plaza, Suite 4510, Boston, MA 02116 ☎ 617/727–3201; fax 617/973–8525; www.massvacation.com.
- Boston National Historical Park Visitor Center ✉ 15 State Street, opposite Old State House ☎ 617/242–5642.
- Boston Common Information Kiosk ✉ Tremont Street ☎ 617/426–3115.
- Cambridge Visitor Information ✉ Harvard Square, Cambridge ☎ 617/497–1630.

GETTING AROUND

Visitor passes

- An MBTA (Massachusetts Bay Transportation Authority) Visitor Pass gives unlimited travel for one, three, or seven days ($6, $11, $22) on all subways, buses, and ferries. It is available at BosTix kiosks (➤ 82), visitor information centres on Boston Common and in the Prudential Center, and North and South stations.

Boats

- ➤ 6 for ferries to the airport.
- MBTA ferry/Boston Harbor cruises (☎ 617/227–4321) link Long Wharf and Charlestown, the Boston Harbor Islands, Salem, and Provincetown.

Buses

- Buses travel farther out into the suburbs than the T, but the T is quicker and easier in the centre.
- Passengers must have the exact change (75¢) or an MTBA Visitor Pass or token.
- For travel farther afield, bus companies operate out of South Station serving destinations throughout New England.

Subway (T)

- Boston's system of subway and elevated trains is known as the T. The four lines—Red, Green, Orange, and Blue—meet in central Boston. "Inbound" and "Outbound" refer to the direction in relation to Park Street Station.
- The T is clean and efficient.
- Trains run from 5AM (later on Sundays) to 12:45AM.
- Tokens ($1) can be bought at station booths. Save time by buying several at once. One token takes you out to the suburbs, but the journey back can cost more.
- Free maps are available at the Park Street Station information booth. Some maps do not show all stops on the Green line branches.

Taxis

- Hail taxis on the street or find them at hotels and taxi stands.
- 24-hour taxi services include: Checker Cab Co ☎ 617/497–9000; Metrocab Cab ☎ 617/242–8000; Town Taxis ☎ 617/536–5000.

Trains

- MBTA commuter trains leave from North Station for destinations west and north, including Lowell, Concord, Salem, Manchester, Gloucester, Rockport, and Ipswich. South Station serves Plymouth and Providence.

DRIVING & CAR RENTAL

Car rental

- Rental drivers must be at least 21; many companies put the minimum age at 25 or charge extra for those aged between 21 and 25.
- Car rental companies include: Avis ☎ 800/331–1212 Budget ☎ 800/527–0700 Dollar ☎ 800/800–4000 Hertz ☎ 800/654–3131.
- Consider using the subway to pick up your car from a rental agency on the outskirts of the city centre.

Driving

- Driving and parking in Boston is a nightmare.
- Park only in legal spots, or you will be towed away. Park in the direction of the traffic.
- Speed limits on the major highways range from 55 to 65mph; elsewhere they range from 30 to 45mph.
- All front seat passengers must wear a seat belt. Children under 12 must sit in the back and use an approved car seat or safety belt.
- You may turn right at a red traffic light if the road ahead is clear.
- Drink/driving laws are very strict. Never drive after drinking; don't keep opened alcohol in the car.

MEDIA & COMMUNICATIONS

Magazines & newspapers

- Free tourist magazines are found in hotel lobbies, and include discount coupons.
- Listings can be found in the *Boston Globe* (Thursday), the *Boston Herald* (Friday), and the *Boston Phoenix* (Thursday; free).
- *Boston Magazine* (monthly) reviews the Boston scene and gives awards to restaurants.

Mail

- Letter boxes are grey/blue and have swing-top lids.

EMERGENCIES

Consulates

- Canada ✉ 3 Copley Place ☎ 617/262–3760
- Great Britain ✉ 600 Atlantic Avenue ☎ 617/248–9555
- Ireland ✉ 535 Boylston Street ☎ 617/267–9330
- Italy ✉ 100 Boylston Street ☎ 617/542–0483
- Portugal ✉ 699 Boylston Street ☎ 617/536–8740
- Spain ✉ 545 Boylston Street ☎ 617/536–2506

Emergency medical treatment

- Ambulance, fire, police ☎ 911
- Massachusetts General Hospital ☎ 617/726–2000
- Inn-House Doctor ☎ 617/859–1776 🕐 24 hours. Makes hotel visits
- Late night pharmacies: CVS ✉ Porter Square (36 White Street, near Massachusetts Avenue), Cambridge ☎ 617/876–5519 🕐 24 hours; ✉ 155 Charles Street, Boston ☎ 617/523–1028 🕐 Until midnight
- Dental emergency ☎ 617/636–6828
- Eye and Ear Infirmary ☎ 617/523–7900
- Physician Referral Service ☎ 617/726–5800 🕐 Mon–Fri 8.30–5

Lost property

- To report lost credit cards: American Express ☎ 800/528–2121; Diners Club/Carte Blanche ☎ 800/234–6377; MasterCard ☎ 800/826–2181; Visa ☎ 800/227–6811.
- To report lost traveller's cheques: American Express ☎ 800/221–7282; Thomas Cook ☎ 800/223–7373.

Index

CityPack
Boston

ABOUT THE AUTHOR
Sue Gordon first got to know Boston as an au pair. Now she is a writer, editor, and garden designer, and visits the city whenever she can. She delights in seeking out corners of the city—and nuggets of information—unknown to her Boston friends.

EDITION REVISERS Sue Gordon and Carolyn Heller
CONTRIBUTIONS TO LIVING BOSTON BY Elizabeth Gehrman and Carolyn Heller
MAPS   © Automobile Association Developments Limited 1997, 1999, 2003
COVER DESIGN   Tigist Getachew, Fabrizio La Rocca

A CIP catalogue record for this book is available from the British Library.

ISBN 0 7495 3567 9

Published by AA Publishing (a trading name of Automobile Association Developments Limited, whose registered office is Millstream, Maidenhead Road, Windsor, Berkshire, SL4 5GD. Registered number 1878835).

© **AUTOMOBILE ASSOCIATION DEVELOPMENTS LIMITED 1997, 1999, 2003**
First published 1997. Reprinted Nov 1998 and Mar 1999. Revised second edition 1999. Reprinted Dec 2000. Revised third edition 2003.

Colour separation by Daylight Colour Art Pte Ltd, Singapore
Printed and bound by Dai Nippon Printing Co (Hong Kong) Ltd.

ACKNOWLEDGMENTS
The Automobile Association would like to thank the following photographers, libraries and associations for their assistance in the preparation of this book: BOSTON ATHENAEUM 41 (Photograph by Peter Vanderwarker). Collection of the Boston Athenaeum); BRIDGEMAN ART LIBRARY 30b Long Branch (detail) by Winslow Homer (1836–1910) Museum of Fine Arts, Boston, Masschusetts; GREATER BOSTON CONVENTION AND VISITORS BUREAU (1-888-SEE-BOSTON) 1b; S GORDON 47t; 53; HARVARD UNIVERSITY ART MUSEUMS 28t (Courtesy of the Fogg Art Museum), 28b Gift of Paul J. Sachs in honour of Edward W. Forbe's 30th year as Director of the Fogg Museum; R HOLMES 27t, 46t; INDEX STOCK IMAGERY/KINDRA CLINEFF 49; JOHN F. KENNEDY LIBRARY & MUSEUM 50b (Robert Schoen); MARY EVANS PICTURE LIBRARY 16r, 17l, 17r; MIT MUSEUMS 53 (The Harold E. Edgerton 1992 Trust); MRI BANKERS GUIDE TO FOREIGN CURRENCY 6; NEW ENGLAND AQUARIUM 48t; 48b; PETER NEWARK'S AMERICAN PICTURES 16l, 17c; OLD SOUTH MEETING HOUSE 42t; STOCKBYTE 5; WORLD PICTURES 52. The remaining picture are held in the Association's own library (AA PHOTO LIBRARY) with contributions from: CHRIS COE cover: State House Dome, back cover: weather vane, 1t, 2, 4, 6tl, 7t, 8cl, 8/9, 9t, 9c, 9r, 10tl, 10cl, 11b, 12t, 12c, 13r, 14t, 15r, 16t, 18tl, 19cr, 20t, 22tl, 22tr, 24tl; ROB HOLMES cover: Period Costume, Giant Milk Bottle, blurred image, 25, 35b, 38b, 42b, 47b, 51b, 54b, 63t, 89t, 89b; JOHN LYNCH 21; MOLLY LYNCH 11t, 20r, 24tc, 26b, 27b, 38t, 62, 63b; JOHN NICHOLSON 12/13, 14l, 19cl, 23tl, 23tr, 24cl, 24cr; CLIVE SAWYER cover: Park Street Church, Back Bay Turret, John Hancock Tower, Old State House, 6tr, 8b, 9b, 10tr, 10cr, 11c, 13t, 15tl, 15tc, 15c, 18tr, 18cl, 18cr, 19t, 20c, 24tr, 26t, 29, 30t, 31t, 31b, 32, 33t, 33b, 34t, 34b, 35t, 36t, 36b, 37, 39, 40, 43, 44t, 44b, 45, 46b, 50t, 51t, 54t, 56, 57, 58, 59, 60, 61; JOHN WILLIAMS 14/15. The author would like to thank the Greater Boston Convention & Visitors Bureau and Ferne Mintz of Bed & Breakfast Agency of Boston.

A01084
Fold out map © Mairs Geographischer Verlag / Falk Verlag, 73751 Ostfildern
Transport map © TCS, Aldershot, England

TITLES IN THE CITYPACK SERIES
• Amsterdam • Bangkok • Barcelona • Beijing • Berlin • Boston • Brussels & Bruges •
• Chicago • Dublin • Florence • Hong Kong • Lisbon • Ljubljana • London • Los Angeles •
• Madrid • Melbourne • Miami • Montréal • Munich • New York • Paris • Prague • Rome •
• San Francisco • Seattle • Shanghai • Singapore • Sydney • Tokyo • Toronto • Venice •
• Vienna • Washington DC •